"*STORY MAPS: TV Drama* is a handy, practical guide that walks writers through the process of creating a compelling TV drama. Using examples from some of the most respected shows on television, writers will learn to master the form from outline to Fade Out. I wish I'd had this book when I was first starting out!"

— Hilary Weisman Graham, Writer, *Bones* (Fox)

"On one hand, I'm thrilled for you that Dan has written this fantastic new book that will undoubtedly help you structure your original TV pilot. On the other hand, I'm furious at him for not writing it a couple of years ago when it could have saved me a ton of brainpower figuring it out for myself. Perhaps one day I'll forgive him. Perhaps not. But the bottom line is, don't learn the hard way like I did. Use Dan's book instead."

— Joe Nimziki, Creator/Executive Producer of upcoming Sony TV series *Kreskin*; Director, *The Howling, Outer Limits*; Senior Executive, New Line Cinema, Sony Pictures and MGM.

"This book blows all others out of the water! There's no other TV writing book that offers this level of detail when it comes to how to structure a one-hour television drama pilot. I wish I had this back when I was breaking in as it would have saved me a lot of time and effort."

— Larry Reitzer, Writer, *Melissa & Joey, My Big Fat Greek Life, Twins, Just Shoot Me!, Ugly Betty*

"I've worked in film and television for years and I can say for certain that there is nothing else like Calvisi's book anywhere out there. His system is truly unique and breaks TV pilot structure down step by step for the first time, using very specific examples from some of the great pilots of recent years. An added bonus is the information about the industry, format and terminology that is clearly explained for the new writer to better understand the scripted television business in Los Angeles."

— Fritz Manger, Producer, *A Deadly Adoption* with Will Ferrell and Kristen Wiig

D1605546

"I've turned to Dan for notes on several feature scripts in the past, and this new book is well-timed as the industry makes a huge shift toward television. The information inside is a fantastic primer in developing a rock-solid one-hour TV pilot. I recommend this book to writers as the foundation in creating excellent story structure."

> — Richard J. Bosner, Producer, *Fruitvale Station, The Wannabe, Other People*

"Daniel Calvisi does an expert job of breaking down the structure of television pilots in a way that's not only easy to understand, but can be easily applied to one's own work. He uses references that are current and offers clear, succinct advice for novice writers which also serves as a great refresher for professionals. If you're thinking of writing a TV pilot, read this book first! It may save you a lot of time in fixing structure problems later."

> — Christine Conradt, Writer/Producer/Director of 50 Lifetime network movies, *The Bride He Bought Online, Stalked at 17, Hotel California, Summer's Moon*

"Dan has a firm grasp on the nature of the one-hour drama for television. I have little doubt that by following his guidelines and doing your homework, he can lead you to create a great pilot of your own!"

> — Jenny Frankfurt, Literary Manager, High Street Management

STORY MAPS: TV Drama:

The Structure of the One-Hour Television Pilot

1st Edition

By

Daniel P. Calvisi

Act Four Screenplays

STORY MAPS: TV Drama: The Structure of the One-Hour Television Pilot

By Daniel P. Calvisi

Published by ACT FOUR SCREENPLAYS

Copyright © Daniel P. Calvisi 2016

ISBN-10: 0-9836266-8-5

ISBN-13: 978-0-9836266-8-8

Cover art by Emir Oručević (www.pulp-art.squarespace.com)

Story Maps on Amazon: http://www.amazon.com/author/danielcalvisi

The TV Pilot Beat Sheet Webinar: http://bit.ly/TVBeatSheet

Work with Dan: ActFourScreenplays.com

For all of the aspiring screenwriters who are working to turn their night job into their day job, their passion into their purpose, and their stories into reality.

For the world builders, the creation machine engineers and the captains of imagination.

For those inspired by the "Golden Age" of scripted television who are now navigating the stormy waters of "Peak TV."

About the Author

Daniel P. Calvisi is a story consultant, screenwriter and the author of *Story Maps: How to Write a GREAT Screenplay*, *Story Maps: 12 Great Screenplays*, and *Story Maps: The Films of Christopher Nolan* (with William Robert Rich). He is a former Story Analyst for major studios like Twentieth Century Fox and Miramax Films. He teaches webinars on writing for film and television with The Writers Store and speaks at writing conferences. He holds a degree in Film and Television from the Tisch School of the Arts at New York University. He lives in Los Angeles. To learn more about Story Maps and how you can work with Dan, visit ActFourScreenplays.com.

TABLE OF CONTENTS

INTRODUCTION

I know there is a great need for this book. I know because I've lost count of the number of writers who have asked me if I had a "Story Map for TV." This trend began a few years ago. Many of the same writers whom I'd coached to write their feature screenplays were now starting to ask about television.

I was hesitant, at first. You see, I've always been a movie guy. I've always focused my writing and story analysis on features, from NYU film school to working as a studio reader and a writing coach to penning books on feature film screenwriting.

Until it hit me that I was watching a LOT more television than film. It was getting bad. Reality shows, too. Not just *Mad Men* or *Curb Your Enthusiasm*, but...*The Real Housewives of New Jersey, Top Chef* and *Unbeatable Banzuke*! (Don't ask.) Too much watching, not enough writing. So I decided to focus only on the good stuff, the best that scripted television had to offer. As you can imagine, my search did not last long, considering the era, the so-called "New Golden Age of Television."

The quality of writing on the small screen is undeniable. It makes perfect sense that countless blogs are dissecting every episode of many shows. TV series are the new novels. There's a ton of writing and analysis out there on the subject of TV writing, but yet, not much that focuses on the details of structure. I searched online for such material but came up empty. I decided to forge my own template, and that process led me to develop this material, which, I surmise, will be of particular interest to feature writers who are planning to write their first pilot.

Whatever your background or goal, please know that this book focuses on <u>the craft</u>, not on career advice. This is not about getting an agent— I'm here as a Story Analyst to dissect great serial television drama to give you a clearer template to guide your own writing. Writing is a solitary and daunting endeavor. I wish for this material to be a lantern to help guide you through the dark tunnel of creation.

Although there is still a lot of quality storytelling out there, I believe that television is at a vital crossroads. We have reached the era of "Peak TV." More shows are being produced and shown on more platforms than ever, and many of the landmark series of recent years have either ended or are coming to the end of their runs. Inevitably, with more content comes more watered-down storytelling. It's time for new worlds, characters, themes and dramatic devices to be introduced by new creative minds from outside the established system. We've had our fill of compelling antiheroes, and the ride has been fun. Their names are iconic: Tony Soprano, Don Draper, Walter White and Dexter Morgan, to name a few. But their time is over.

Your time has just begun. So start that pilot <u>today</u>, not tomorrow, because we need your voice on TV. But remember one thing...

Just as we know from writing movies, the same is true of television: You can only reinvent the form once you know the form. Once you know the past, you can create the future: The next, great Golden Age of television.

Good luck and happy writing,

Dan Calvisi

For those of you who are new to the landscape of television writing in Hollywood, let's review some important concepts and terms...

Creator...Writer...STAR?

In television, writers enjoy more prominence in the creative process than they do in studio films. Most producers on a show are also writers. There also tends to be more women writers in TV than in film, and there is a defined ladder of succession from Writer's Assistant to Executive Producer.

The writing staff of a show is managed by a Showrunner, who is often the creator of the show who also wrote the pilot, and is essentially the creative force that steers the ship. The Showrunner is to TV what the Director is to film.

In recent years, several Showrunners have become celebrities themselves; building fanbases on the Internet and on talk shows. You can follow many Showrunners and TV writers on Twitter.

David Benioff began as a novelist, moved to features and became co-Showrunner of *Game of Thrones*

Shonda Rhimes, creator of *Grey's Anatomy, Scandal* and *How To Get Away with Murder*

CONTENT IS KING!

There are more channels and platforms that distribute scripted content than ever. Many cable channels that were established with documentary/reality shows are now focused on scripted content, and websites are buying pitches and pilots every day. Even cable delivery services like DirectTV and video gaming platforms like Xbox and PlayStation are producing original content.

Before you begin writing your pilot, consider the landscape and how your show may fit within it. You must first know the players, and then do your research to find out their individual "brand," which often corresponds with their target demographic, or audience. (E.g., Freeform, formerly ABC Family, targets tween and teen girls, so don't bother submitting your serial killer procedural to them.) These are the most active networks in the United States:

"Broadcast" Networks: ABC, CBS, NBC and FOX

"Premium" Cable Networks: HBO, SHOWTIME, STARZ, CINEMAX

"Basic" Cable Networks: A&E, AMC, BRAVO, COMEDY CENTRAL, DISCOVERY, DISNEY, DISNEY XD, FREEFORM, FX, FXX, HISTORY, IFC, MTV, NICKELODEON, TBS, TNT, SUNDANCE, USA, WGN

Internet: Netflix, Amazon, Hulu, YouTube, Yahoo, AOL, MSN, Crackle

That's not even a complete list.

Keep in mind that the networks listed above are not always the production companies that make the shows. For example, Lionsgate Television produced *Mad Men*, which aired on AMC.

Core Formats

There are very specific formats for scripted shows on U.S. television. You must know the differences in formats to decide which type of show you plan to write.

1-Hour Drama/Dramedy: A 60-minute show with or without commercials. (*Game of Thrones, The Good Wife, Homeland*)

30-Minute Single-Camera Sitcom: A comedy shot like a movie. (*The Office, Curb Your Enthusiasm, New Girl, Veep*)

30-Minute Multi-Camera Sitcom: A sitcom that uses a laugh track. Shot mostly in a studio, perhaps in front of a live audience. (*Two Broke Girls, How I Met Your Mother, The Big Bang Theory*)

30-Minute Dramedy Hybrid: We're seeing more shows in the 30-minute running time that use a unique mix of drama and comedy. *Transparent* and *Girls* are notable examples.

Web Series: A short form narrative video series. Length varies, but 3-8 minutes per episode is a common range. Webisodes are often used as pitch reels to sell a longer-form series. (*Hulu, YouTube, Crackle*)

In this book, we will focus on the **1-Hour Drama/Dramedy**.

Procedural vs. Serial

A **procedural** series is one that consists of self-contained or stand-alone stories. Each episode introduces a specific dramatic dilemma that the characters must solve by the end of the episode. This is also known as "case-of-the-week." In a procedural, the weekly case is the focus, while the ongoing arcs and themes, if any, are secondary. Common procedurals are police, lawyer, and medical dramas such as *CSI, Chicago PD, Grey's Anatomy,* etc.

A **serial or serialized show** is one that comprises overarching storylines/character arcs that develop over the course of the season or series. These ongoing stories and themes take precedent and build towards a gradual climax. While serialized TV shows can contain "case-of-the-week'" stories, they are often secondary and used instead to explore/reflect the larger story/themes. They build and explore a sprawling world filled with a long list of characters who shift in and out of the spotlight. Serialized TV shows are best aired and viewed in narrative order to prevent viewers from becoming confused and losing pace with plot developments. These shows perform well on DVR, DVD and streaming, which allow fans to watch at their own pace. Examples would be *Lost, Mad Men, The Walking Dead* and most premium-cable dramas like *Game of Thrones* and *Homeland*.

Serial/Procedural Hybrids are also a popular form, and can vary in their construction. This usually means that a show will alternate between a case-of-the-week episode and a "mythology" episode that advances a long term narrative arc. A classic example of this form would be *The X-Files*, which alternated between "monster-of-the-week" episodes and episodes about the ongoing saga of the Smoking Man and a potential alien invasion (which also tied into Fox Mulder's backstory with his missing sister). Like many hybrid shows, the mythology became more dominant as the series went on. A hybrid show can also combine a case and mythology in a single episode, as in many episodes of *Dexter*, where Dexter Morgan hunts a new target and he evades his sister or others as they get closer to learning his deadly secret.

Pilot vs. Spec

A "pilot" script is an original screenplay for the first episode of a series. **A great pilot script is the only firm requirement to break into the business of writing television.**

A "spec" script is an original episode of an existing show, written as a writing sample to show that you can write in a specific genre and within an established set of dramatic parameters. As TV shows are written by a writing staff, it's important to show that you can be a team player and write effectively in someone else's voice. Specs are not written as commonly these days by aspiring writers, but are sometimes requested as writing samples after a writer gets noticed for an original pilot. At the least, it's good practice to write in your intended genre; e.g., if you want to write one-hour crime procedurals, then you could write a spec episode of *Criminal Minds* (or whatever the current incarnation of *Criminal Minds* may be). Keep in mind that a TV spec is different than a feature spec.

"Premise" Pilot vs. "3rd Episode" Pilot

The term "premise pilot" denotes a pilot that takes the entire script to fully set up the story that will be continued in future episodes. The structure of the pilot does not represent the structure of a regular episode of the series. *The Walking Dead* is an example of a premise pilot; there is a lot of ground to cover in setting up the zombie-infested world, so Rick Grimes is the "newborn" who takes us through it. He is the audience's surrogate—we discover this new world as he does. In future episodes, he has met up with other survivors and they must tackle problems as a group.

On the contrary, a pilot that throws us into the action, with the premise already set up, is often called a "third episode," as in it uses the same structure as the third episode would use, when the series engine is established. *Scandal* is an example of a third episode pilot; Olivia Pope and her employees are already well-seasoned in what they do, and we are brought up to speed quickly. The case-of-the-week begins six minutes into the pilot when Lt. Colonel Sully walks into Olivia's agency, covered in blood, and says he didn't kill his girlfriend. If *Scandal* was a premise pilot, we may have opened with Olivia Pope graduating law school and taking her first job, and maybe Act One would end with her opening up her own firm.

No matter which type of pilot you write, it always helps to <u>begin the story as soon as possible</u>. Cut out anything that only exists as setup or exposition without advancing the central throughline of the episode. **Enter the action of your story as late as possible in the *world* but as soon as possible in the *script*.** Does that make sense? Think of it like this: if your world is homicide detectives in New York City, do you begin the story in the police academy or once our protagonist is already on the job? Do you open on them getting coffee at Starbucks or walking into a luxury loft where a beat cop ushers them to the dead body on the kitchen floor? In both cases, I'd go with the latter option, unless the former option can be written so as to immediately advance the present line of action.

There's no time to waste. The reader is anxious. Get to the good stuff ASAP.

It should be noted that in the original pilot script for "Scandal," Sully walks into the agency on page 12, which would have corresponded to 12 minutes into the episode. They wisely moved up this Inciting Incident for the actual episode to minute six, getting the case started in half the time.

Most competent rewrites trim the fat and get the story moving quicker, while maintaining the same essential beats and character moments in the first couple acts. They just do it with fewer words, which just so happens to be one of the central skills of the experienced screenwriter.

YOUR PILOT

A FASCINATING PROTAGONIST

Every TV series begins with a compelling character. Your main character, the protagonist, is the anchor of the show. Your leading woman or man must be someone that we really want to spend time with. A lot of time, maybe even years, if the show is a hit. That's a big time commitment for a viewer! So make your hero worth the investment. Make them fascinating.

Let's look at some of the characteristics of a strong TV protagonist.

Hero/Anti-Hero/Newborn/Fish out of Water: Which archetype best fits your protagonist? A hero is someone we root for because they always try to do the right thing (Raylan Givens in *Justified*). An Anti-Hero is someone we root for despite them doing horrible things for selfish reasons (Frank Underwood in *House of Cards*). A Newborn is someone who has just entered a new world which they will show they are fit for (Rick in *The Walking Dead*). A Fish out of Water is someone who represents the polar opposite of the new dramatic territory they find themselves in (Daenarys in *Game of Thrones*).

Ordinary/Extraordinary: Is your protagonist an ordinary schmuck who's been thrown into the deep end of the pool and must sink or swim...or a skilled operator (a "specialist") who does things we can only dream about? The best protagonists are both, like Walter White of *Breaking Bad*, an ordinary chemistry teacher who uses his exceptional science skills to become a major force in the drug trade.

Skill: What are they good at? They must be good at *something*, even if they're a loser. Even the character we love to laugh at should get a win every now and then.

Redemption Arc: We always want to watch a character struggle to redeem themselves for past sins or to recover from past abuses. The quintessential example of this is Don Draper in *Mad Men*.

External and Internal Goal: Your protagonist must have something interesting to do in terms of a physical goal and an emotional need and they must take action to achieve these goals. These two goals may form the "A" and "B" stories of your pilot and generate perennial lines of action for the series.

Identifiable ("Rooting Interest"): We don't have to fully understand or relate to your protagonist, but there should be some reason that we root for them to achieve their goal.

Misbehavior: It's fun to give your protagonist a trait that consistently creates problems for them. A quirk or compulsion. Obsessive-compulsive disorder, sexism, a short fuse, ego, etc.

Fatal Flaw: This is their worst trait, their Achilles Heel, the blind side that threatens to ruin them. It can be a personality trait, like anger or racism, or an element of backstory, like Don Draper's true identity as Dick Whitman or Jon Snow's sense of inadequacy for being the bastard son of Ned Stark.

Assumption of Power: We want to see our hero realize their own true power and unleash a show of strength that makes them come into their own. They take off the mask, throw down the gauntlet, find their courage – however you may label it, I think you need this moment in your pilot and also at the end of each season, if not in every episode.

Identity: Most shows today develop a strong theme of identity around their protagonists. What it means to be a man or woman in society...status... morality...living by a personal "code," etc. These are all themes that relate to what kind of person our hero yearns to be. Think of the arcs of Walter White in *Breaking Bad*, Jack in *Lost* and Ned Stark in the first season of *Game of Thrones*. Television is a particularly good medium to explore this theme as we will be watching this character's personal growth over a span of years (except for poor Ned).

Dynamic Ally: Every protagonist needs a best friend or helper who is going to stick around for the long haul. A character who represents the major ally/champion/partner-in-crime of the protagonist and helps to facilitate change in the protagonist.

Shadow: This is a supporting character who represents the polar opposite of our protagonist, always lurking and always creating conflict.

Let's look at some fascinating TV personalities, captured in a list of elements that are vital to creating a three-dimensional dramatic character.

Rustin Cohle (*True Detective*)

Defining Characteristic: Pessimistic

Skill: Obsessive

Misbehavior: Abrasive/Iconoclastic

Achilles Heel/Flaw: His daughter's death

External Goal: To solve the case

Internal Goal: To find peace with the universe

Dynamic Ally & Shadow: Detective Martin Hart

Pilot Arc: From space cadet to good detective

First Season Arc: From haunted to peaceful

Series Arc: None*

*The Cohle/Hart *True Detective* series only lasted one season.

Walter White
(*Breaking Bad*)

Defining Characteristic: Controlling

Skill: Chemistry

Misbehavior: Entitlement

Achilles Heel: His family and his lust for power

External Goal: To become a drug lord

Internal Goal: To protect his family/ To get his due

Dynamic Ally*: Jesse Pinkman

Shadow*: Hank, his brother-in-law

Pilot Arc: From a wimpy chemistry teacher to a successful meth cooker

First Season Arc: Walt develops his signature blue meth and facilitates a distribution deal with a dangerous gangster

Series Arc: Cancer-ridden loser to sociopathic drug baron

*See the note in Act One of my *Breaking Bad* pilot map in **Case Studies**, in regards to how Hank and Jesse's functions flip as the series goes on.

Senator Francis "Frank" Underwood
(*House of Cards*)

Defining Characteristic: Manipulative

Skill: Cunning

Misbehavior: Unethical (often expressed in comedic asides)

Achilles Heel/Flaw: Hubris

External Goal: To win high office

Internal Goal: To please his wife

Dynamic Ally: Peter Russo

Shadow: Zoe Barnes, cub reporter

Pilot Arc: Low-level politician to rising star

First Season Arc: Frank becomes Vice President

Series Arc: We shall see!

In the *Mad Men* pilot, Peggy Olson is the "New Arrival," but as the series progresses, she will become a secondary protagonist to Don Draper's primary protagonist. Here are her Basic elements for the series.

Peggy Olson (*Mad Men*)

Defining Characteristic: Workaholic

Skill: Writing advertising campaigns

Misbehavior: Chooses job over relationships

Achilles Heel/Flaw: Needs Don's validation

External Goal: To make it in a man's world

Internal Goal: To find love

Dynamic Ally: Don

Shadow: Joan

Pilot Arc: From mousy innocent to sexual woman

First Season Arc: From secretary to copywriter

Series Arc: From newbie to experienced professional

THEME

What is your show about? Why are you telling this story? What emotions and ideas do you plan to explore? What should your characters *do*? These questions point to theme.

You can and should use your theme/s to inspire stories, scenes and character arcs. Theme can act as a "control" to focus your stories.

Mad Men's central theme is *the pursuit of happiness in an increasingly cynical and chaotic world*, with key sub-themes explored along the way (sexism, racism, status, family, etc.). The show is a great example of exploring the same key themes over several seasons. From the beginning, the decision to set the story in New York City in the 1960s, a place and time of great societal change, practically guaranteed the exploration of certain themes, such as issues of race, gender, age and class. And specifying it to the advertising industry necessitated an examination of pop culture, artifice, creativity versus commerce, and identity.

One can see how the original cast of characters sprung from these themes. Imagine series creator Matthew Weiner sitting down to first outline the series, knowing only the central theme, the time period and the setting. The goal, as always, is conflict and contrast. It quickly crystallizes that the women on the show (Peggy, Joan, Betty) will be dealing with chauvinism in the workplace, sexual freedom and the balance of family and career as the ideal 1950s housewife image breaks down. The men at the ad agency should be divided into two basic camps: the old guard (Burt, Roger, Don) and the young Turks (Pete, Ken, Harry). The old guys bring the experiences of The Great Depression, war and conservative values, and the young men struggle to find themselves in the void stuck between their father's black-and-white world and the shifting morals and influences of their evolving generation. Then you've got the stratification between class and money, and the impact of the creative spirit on daily life. Pete Campbell comes from money, whereas Don Draper comes from a dirt-poor existence. Pete has reached his position in the company almost solely on his family name, while Don *created* his persona from whole cloth.

In *Breaking Bad*, the theme of *sacrifice* comes into play time and time again as Walter White keeps being put in impossible situations where he must decide what and who he is willing to sacrifice to save his own skin. As Walt falls deeper and deeper into the criminal underworld, the question of *survival* comes up in almost every episode. And he can't just leave the criminal life, because he has inoperable cancer, so it's literally a struggle for life and death.

The short opening sequence for the pilot of *The Walking Dead* drives home the central theme of the entire series – when Rick makes the terrible decision to shoot the little girl zombie in the head, he is struggling with *how to maintain his humanity in the wake of disaster*. Each episode of the series will force the characters to deal with this theme.

In the *Scandal* pilot, the theme shifts and sharpens over time. It begins focused on *truth*, best exemplified by Olivia's use of her gut instinct. She believes her instinct alone can determine if someone is lying or not. It never fails her. But soon we meet the one man who can cloud that instinct: her former lover, President Fitzgerald Grant. Olivia begins to see her client's dilemma mirroring her own—Sully can beat the murder charges if he only admits to his true love for another man. But in doing so, he will destroy his career and carefully-crafted persona. Same goes for Olivia and her secret relationship with Grant. It is at this point in the pilot script that the theme begins to focus into *the sacrifices we make for true love*. The integration of plot, theme and the protagonist's character arc is seamless.

True Detective's pilot is split between two time periods: 1995 and 2012. We begin in 2012 as Detective Martin Hart is interviewed about his partner, Rustin Cohle. Hart is examining what makes the man, starting by expounding on what makes a good cop. The relationship between these two men and the examination of their true nature, *not* the Dora Lange murder case, is the "A" story of the pilot and the season. The central theme is right there in the title: *What makes a "true" detective?*

COMPELLING CRISIS

"What's the concept?" is a question you hear often in the world of features, but in television, it's not so simple. The "concept" is not just one story. It's a set of characters, a launching pad, and an ongoing engine that generates many stories. A TV series must have a central conflict that is inherently fascinating, rife with high stakes and requires significant time to solve. Let's call this a "Compelling Crisis."

The Compelling Crisis is not always the central conflict of each episode. For example, on *Lost*, the Compelling Crisis is a group of people trying to escape a mysterious island filled with dangerous, supernatural occurrences. But an individual episode of the series would be driven by a smaller, unique "story engine" that is a variation on the Compelling Crisis, like "They must rescue three of their friends from the secret hatch before one of their enemy captives escapes and signals an attack on their camp."

No matter how clever or outlandish your scenario, it will not be compelling to an audience without characters we can invest in and root for. Notice how all of these crises flow from character:

Breaking Bad: A mild-mannered high school teacher becomes a drug lord under the nose of his brother-in-law, a DEA agent.

Downton Abbey: A wealthy British lord struggles to keep his estate and antiquated ways as the unrelenting pressure of the 20th century threatens to tear it, and his family, apart.

Mad Men: An ad man with a dark secret desperately struggles for happiness in the turbulent 1960s.

Sons of Anarchy: "Hamlet in a biker gang." Stepfather and son fight to keep a gun-running biker gang together amidst corruption, betrayals and escalating violence.

The Americans: Two Russian sleeper agents in the 1980s pose as the perfect suburban couple by day as they run missions by night, which ironically bring them closer as real lovers.

SETTING/WORLD

An English manor at the dawn of World War I...Manhattan in the 1960s...a motorcycle club. These are the "worlds" these stories live in.

A great show takes us into a world that we've never visited, or, at least, haven't seen portrayed quite like this. The world will invariably be a strong part of the Compelling Crisis. Here are some of the more fascinating worlds of recent television history:

Boardwalk Empire: Prohibition-era New Jersey shore

Game of Thrones: The fantasy world of Westeros

Homeland: The inner workings of the CIA

House of Cards: Backrooms of Washington, D.C.

Justified: Backwater Kentucky

The Walking Dead: Post-zombie apocalypse America

REGENERATING STORY ENGINE
(a.k.a. "100 EPISODES OR BUST!")

100 episodes is the magic number in which a show goes into syndication (cha-ching!), thus it is the goal of every series.

Think about how your series can sustain 100 hours of narrative. You don't need an outline of all 100 episodes, but it's good to have an answer when you're asked a question like, "What happens at the end of season two?" It's helpful to know where the first few seasons will begin and end, for your own use and to convince other professionals that you really know your series.

It's time to put that Compelling Crisis into action. To narrow in on the core of your story—<u>what it is</u>. What drives each episode. What makes it drama and what we tune in to see each week. In simple terms, you must identify...

THE "WEEK-TO-WEEK"

Let's get in our time machine and eavesdrop on some conversations at networks around town...

Okay, I get it that this series is about a chemistry teacher who starts to make meth, but what does he DO each week?

So this guy is a creative director at an ad agency in the Sixties – what happens each episode? We watch him sit around and create ad campaigns in bell-bottoms?

So, her husband the politician cheated on her and she's back to work as a lawyer. Does she work on a new case each week or is it the same case for the whole season? Does she go to trial or stay in the office? When she was still a wife, would you have called her a good one or a bad one?

That last question may be a stretch, but you can see what these hypothetical network types are asking: what happens each week? After all, 10 different writers could be handed the concept of an ensemble drama within the wealthy British upper class at the dawn of World War I and come back with 10 different takes. It took Julian Fellowes' unique approach to make this idea into the brilliant character study that is *Downton Abbey*.

The Week-to-Week also addresses a pivotal part of any show: the audience. What will they see and how will they feel? Here is my estimation of the Week-to-Week for three of our sample shows:

Scandal: Olivia Pope and her team solve a crisis for a client that mirrors her/their personal struggles.

The Walking Dead: Rick and the survivors deal with a new threat from the zombies and their fellow humans.

True Detective (Season 1): Cohle and Hart use more extreme measures to pursue the case as their personal lives go further off the rails.

Keep in mind that a "premise pilot" may not utilize the Week-to-Week engine of subsequent episodes. For example, the Week-to-Week of *The Walking Dead* hinges on Rick's interaction with his fellow survivors, but in the pilot, he has not yet met up with them. When you look at the beat sheets for our sample pilots (in **Case Studies**), try to determine if the pilot utilizes the same Week-to-Week engine as future episodes. (You'll have to be familiar with the show to do this.)

It should also be noted that heavily serialized shows may not even have a defined Week-to-Week structure. They will always have familiar devices, like in *Game of Thrones* it seems like someone is often being taken hostage, or in *Mad Men* they often present ad campaigns to clients. But those things don't *always* happen. There is no way to predict which characters or plots will be focused on in each episode.

This is why it can be especially difficult to pitch a serialized show: it's hard for someone else to "get" the Week-to-Week. (But nothing's easy to sell in Hollywood, so just write a show *you* would watch.)

Where and how you begin your pilot is a crucial decision, considering that your opening pages are your first and only chance to grab the reader. So think long and hard about how you will bring the reader into the world of your story.

You may want to utilize a framing device, like in *True Detective* with the interviews with Cohle and Hart in 2012, which prompt flashbacks to 1995 and 2002. The interviews establish the context for the time jumps, as well as provide key exposition.

Your way in may be through a character. In *Scandal*, Quinn, the new hire at Olivia Pope's crisis management firm, is the Newborn who acts as our proxy to get crucial exposition.

Consider a high-energy, high-stakes opening scene to really grab your reader. We'll never forget the explosive Teasers of our favorite shows: Sheriff Rick Grimes having to shoot a zombie child in *The Walking Dead*. Walter "Underwear Man" White crashing his RV in the desert in *Breaking Bad*. The plane crash sequence that opens *Lost*.

However you open your pilot, just make sure you get to the story as soon as possible. The only person more anxious than the viewer is the industry reader. I know, because I've spent years being both!

SEASONAL ARCS

A TV season used to last 24-26 episodes. New episodes, interspersed with the occasional re-run (remember that term?), stretched the TV season from fall to early summer. As a viewer, by the time you got to May sweeps, you probably couldn't remember how the season began in September, so techniques like subtle callbacks and bookending were not very effective.

Today, only "broadcast" network (ABC, CBS, NBC, FOX) shows air over 20 episodes in a season. Outside of them, drama series seasons tend to be in the 10-13 episode range and new episodes air each week until the season concludes, creating an unbroken block of "appointment" television. If the network even airs re-runs, they will often save them for a marathon to precede the next season's opener. If the series is an original from a streaming service like Netflix, then an entire season is made available at the same time. DVRs and streaming have made "binge" viewing and repeated viewings easier, so viewers are scrutinizing their favorite shows more than ever, and looking at each season as a whole.

Great series come up with new scenarios and settings for each season that brilliantly continue the Compelling Crisis but with higher stakes, a new setting and a unique threat.

Downton Abbey Season one ended with the declaration of World War I, so season two begins in a trench battle and deals with the effects of the war upon the Abbey.

Mad Men Each season finds Don with a new mistress and a new threat to his secret identity. The time period advances, bringing with it new societal pressure and changes in the ad agency.

Lost I had grown weary of *Lost* until they started using the "flash forwards" in season four that showed how the survivors got off the island. This device, coupled with the Showrunners' announcement that the sixth season would be the show's last, injected a new level of urgency into the show.

Friday Night Lights The third season saw the coach pushed out of the comfortable West Side and forced to take a job on the East Side, where the football program had no money and a weak bench.

Dexter Each season of Dexter introduced a "dynamic ally/villain" who learned Dexter's secret and either wanted to kill him or join him. The Trinity Killer (John Lithgow) in season four and Lumen (Julia Stiles) in season five are good examples of this device.

SERIES ARCS

The best dramas also offer a steep arc of change over the length of the series. This may take the form of slowly answering a major dramatic question (*What is the island?*) or showing us the steps leading up to an inevitable end (On *Downton Abbey*, we always knew that their age of pomp and circumstance could not last.). The most interesting relationship in *Justified* was that of lawman Raylan Givens and his perpetual nemesis, Boyd Crowder. Fittingly, the series ended with a conversation between the two men, separated by glass, with Boyd clad in prison orange.

In some cases, the creators know from the get-go how the series will end, and in others, they're basically making it up as they go along. With *Breaking Bad*, Vince Gilligan's plan from the start was for Walter White to go from "Mr. Chips to Scarface," although Gilligan has said in interviews that they often wrote Walter White into a corner without knowing how they were going to get him out. *Mad Men* begins in 1960 with Don Draper struggling to come up with a campaign for cigarettes and ends in 1970 with him creating one of the most famous commercials in history, for Coca Cola.

You don't have to know the arc of your entire series, but it can't hurt.

THE TV DRAMA
STORY MAP

The Story Map is a method of constructing and deconstructing a narrative that I originally developed working as a Story Analyst for major studios and production companies and honed over time as I worked with hundreds of writers as a consultant.

This is how professional screenwriters structure their scripts, and in mapping an existing TV series, you can best see how they did it. The story map reveals the building blocks of the narrative. It's how modern shows are structured and paced, so your script should reflect this structure and pace on the page. If shows are edited this way, then your screenplay should be edited this way as well, so you suck in the reader and give them the experience of an audience member watching your show.

I always advocate the use of outlines before you begin to write screenplay pages, and the Story Map is the ultimate outline template. This is _form_, not formula. It does not dictate your story choices; it merely offers a tried-and-true framework to hold your unique characters and plotting. You can use the map to solve story problems _before_ you begin to write pages, saving you months of work and cutting out several ineffective drafts. The amount of detail you fill into your map is up to you, but you should fill in at least a few words in each category. The goal is to create a roadmap to follow as you write, ultimately making the writing process that much easier.

I separate the map into the "Basic" and "Full" Story Maps. The Basic map compiles the main dramatic elements of the story with a focus on your protagonist, and the Full map breaks down the major "signpost" beats of the plot. Let's start with...

THE "BASIC" STORY MAP

The Basic Story Map collects many of the elements discussed earlier in this book, like your Compelling Crisis, World, and Theme, and puts them in one place for easy reference. If your story is a house, the Basic Story Map is the foundation.

We already looked at partial Basic maps (in **A Fascinating Protagonist**) for protagonists from *True Detective, Mad Men, Breaking Bad* and *House of Cards*. Now, let's look at the complete Basic Story Map for the pilot of *Scandal*.

As previously mentioned, *Scandal* is a "third episode" pilot so the Week-to-Week is already in place and will not change once we progress past the pilot (at least for the first season. In subsequent seasons, *Scandal* became increasingly serialized, focusing on the main characters' struggles rather than the "case of the week," which is a common practice these days. But for our purposes, we will remain focused on the pilot.). In the case of a "premise" pilot like *The Walking Dead*, the Week-to-Week is not yet clear in the first hour.

Scandal BASIC STORY MAP

TITLE: *SCANDAL*

THEME: Recognizing and sacrificing for true love

COMPELLING CRISIS: Olivia Pope works in the shadows fixing others' problems but she can't fix her secret affair with the most publicly visible man in the world.

WEEK-TO-WEEK: Olivia Pope and her team solve a crisis for a client that mirrors her/their personal struggles.

WORLD: Crisis Management in Washington, D.C.

PROTAGONIST: OLIVIA POPE

DEFINING CHARACTERISTIC: Tough

SKILL: Her gut instinct

MISBEHAVIOR: Denies her own problems

ACHILLES HEEL/FLAW: Her love for the President

EXTERNAL GOAL: To prove Sully's innocence

INTERNAL GOAL: To stand up to the President

CENTRAL CONFLICT/ANTAGONIST: Sully and the President

DYNAMIC ALLY: Quinn

SHADOW: President Fitzgerald Grant

ENDING: Olivia inspires Sully to come clean and she decides to take on Grant.

PILOT ARC: From cold and in control, to weak and vulnerable, to back in control.

You can use the **Story Map Worksheet** in the **Appendix** to define these crucial elements for your pilot. Don't be afraid to change them at any time as your story comes into focus.

1-HOUR TV DRAMA BASIC STRUCTURE

There is a standard narrative template used in the television industry that you can use to help guide you as you write your original pilot. From this point forward, I will be focusing mainly on the pilot episodes of *Scandal, True Detective, The Walking Dead, Game of Thrones, Mad Men, House of Cards, Mr. Robot* and *Breaking Bad*, but I encourage you to map your favorite shows to better understand their structure.

The Basics:

4-6 Acts: As you can see in "TV Script Lengths" below, many shows choose to call the first act a "Teaser." Whatever the case, a one-hour drama screenplay is going to be broken into 4-6 acts in total. These act breaks roughly correspond to commercial breaks on advertising-driven networks.

54-60 pages total: My recent research reveals that most pilots fall into this page range. Established writers often turn in longer pilots, but I suggest you try not to go over 60 pages.

A, B & C story: There should be at least two plot threads in your pilot—these are referred to as your "A" and "B" stories. It's up to you if you want to add a C, D or more. Each "story" represents a <u>line of action</u>, which is a character pursuing a goal with a beginning, middle and end.

One of the most crucial decisions you will make is how many characters and stories to introduce in your pilot. If you cram too many in, it will feel too dense, and if you focus on too few, then the reader won't get the sense of a bigger story that can sustain 100 episodes. You want a great ending, but it can't pay off *everything*, otherwise it will feel too complete or "closed-ended"—like a feature—so you need to leave us hanging to some degree and wanting more. It sounds difficult, because it is! This is a balancing act that every first-time TV writer must learn how to manage.

Cliffhangers: You don't want your viewers turning the channel or your readers dropping your script, so it's imperative that each act (and, ideally, each scene) leaves us wanting to find out what happens next.

There should consistently be some sense of escalation of conflict/stakes, a surprising turn in direction or a new mystery to be solved. The end of an act is often referred to as an "Act-Out."

TELEVISION SCRIPT FORMAT

A quick note on format. The basic formatting elements of a one-hour TV drama are essentially the same as that of a feature screenplay. Scene headings, action/description, dialogue, transitions, etc. are treated the same in a scriptwriting software program like Final Draft, but there are a few key differences.

The most important difference highlights why a 4-6 act structure is so important to TV: the writer actually labels each act in a TV script.

If you're going to point out to a reader where you're placing your act breaks, then you better be absolutely sure you're placing them correctly! There is no place to hide.

Unlike in feature screenplays, each act is labeled and usually preceded by a page break. For example, here's the break from <u>ACT ONE</u> to <u>ACT TWO</u> in a hypothetical sample script (that may or may not be inspired by an actual show). Notice the underlined act markers and the page break in-between Act One and Act Two.

```
Rick FIRES his Magnum, splitting the noggin of a
Walker like a ripe grapefruit, or, at least, a
grapefruit that happens to be filled with blood
and brains.


                    END OF ACT ONE
```

                    ACT TWO

INT. PRISON - DAY

Rick plays air hockey with Carl.

                    CARL
          Should we be wasting generator
          power on air hockey?

I've seen some pilot scripts that did not bother with a page break after the end of an act, and I honestly thought they looked crowded, like the writer was trying to "cheat" and cram more in than they should. Tactics like this (using really small margins is another classic scam) are immediately obvious to a seasoned reader and mark you as an amateur.

It should be noted that many pilots written for pay-cable networks like HBO do not use act markers or page breaks. These pilot scripts are written pretty much just like a feature, albeit with fewer pages (feature screenplays generally run in the 100-110 page range). The scripts for *True Detective, House of Cards* and *Mad Men* do not label act breaks, although *Mad Men* contains FADE OUTs where conventional act breaks would go.

Even if the writers do not insert act break markers, a pilot script is almost always going to be structured in the conventional 4-6 act template.

As with feature screenplays, a properly formatted teleplay page should roughly equate to one minute of screen time. One page = one minute. Thus, a script for a one-hour drama should max out around 60 pages. The current sweet spot for one-hour pilot scripts seems to be in the range of 54-58 pages.

Keep in mind that although an average episode on an ad-driven network minus commercials runs only 45-48 minutes, pilot scripts must be longer, at least 50 pages. It is assumed that if it goes to camera, cutting and trimming will be done in post-production. It's always better to have too much story rather than too little (but try not to exceed 60 pages).

I've seen some pilots from proven show creators that run 70-plus pages, but their long résumé allows them to get away with it. New writers need to prove they can write a concise, active pilot in the industry-standard page range.

TV Script Lengths

There are standard page ranges for each act. For reference, I've listed the page ranges of some notable pilots below. These breakdowns are taken from <u>the scripts</u>, not the aired episodes. Notice the variations and the similarities in the ranges.

The Blacklist (NBC) Pilot: Jon Bokenkamp	**Bates Motel (**A&E) Pilot: Cuse, Ehrin and Cipriano
Teaser: 1-12	Teaser: 1-8
Act One: 13-21	Act One: 9-22
Act Two: 22-28	Act Two: 23-39
Act Three: 29-38	Act Three: 40-52
Act Four: 39-44	Act Four: 53-58
Act Five: 45-57	Act Five: 59-60
The Good Wife (CBS) Pilot: King & King	**Devious Maids** (Lifetime) Pilot: Marc Cherry
Teaser: 1-16	Teaser: 1-4
Act One: 17-29	Act One: 5-18
Act Two: 30-44	Act Two: 19-30
Act Three: 45-54	Act Three: 31-39
Act Four: 55-64	Act Four: 40-52
Sleepy Hollow (FOX) Pilot: Kurtzman & Orci & Iscove	**Extant** (CBS) Pilot: Mickey Fisher
Act One: 1-14	Act One: 1-12
Act Two: 15-30	Act Two: 13-30
Act Three: 31-40	Act Three: 31-43
Act Four: 41-47	Act Four: 44-56
Act Five: 48-62	Act Five: 53-58

Looking at the page ranges above, you can see that it is the individual choice of each writer on how they want to break up their story. One writer chooses to label the first act a "Teaser," whereas another labels it "Act One." A "Teaser plus four" structure is essentially the same as a five act structure; it's up to the writer how they want to present the material. The writers of "Bates Motel" chose to label the last two pages as "Act Five," whereas they could have easily just tacked them on to the end of Act Four. (In sitcom scripts, a short epilogue or wrap-up scene is often labeled a "Tag.")

There is no absolute right or wrong way to break up your pilot script into Acts, but again, I suggest you stick to the general page ranges above, which are understood and implemented by most professional TV writers. If you turn in a script with 16 acts, you will mark yourself as an amateur.

How do you decide which act structure will work best with your pilot? The best way is to find an existing series that is similar to yours in tone, genre, material, audience or any other factor you deem important, and use it as a structural template for your pilot. If you can't find the actual pilot script, watch the pilot episode and write up a scene list. (When pitching your pilot, you may refer to this template show as your "comp," so the other party can see how your series can easily fall into current programming habits. For example, if your pilot is a legal thriller about a female lawyer, then you could cite *The Good Wife* as your "comp." It should go without saying that you should only cite successful shows as comps!)

Break down a few episodes of your "comp" with the **Story Map Worksheet** in the **Appendix** and use the map to guide you as you beat out your own pilot. You don't have to stick to this structure forever, but it can be a good guide for your first pass.

If you're already thinking ahead to future episodes, keep in mind that a series often sticks to the same general act structure and page ranges used in the pilot. For example, look at how closely the pilot script of *Breaking Bad* compares to a script from its third season:

Breaking Bad Pilot:	**Breaking Bad** #308:
Teaser: 1-3	Teaser: 1-4
Act One: 4-17	Act One: 5-15
Act Two: 18-31	Act Two: 16-31
Act Three: 32-43	Act Three: 32-42
Act Four: 44-57	Act Four: 43-53

Does this structural template feel restrictive and formulaic to you? Keep in mind this similarity in page ranges is <u>form</u>, not formula. It does not dictate the writer's creative choices, just the length of the structure that the scenes are "poured into." This may seem restrictive to the novice, but it is actually challenging, liberating and allows for greater productivity to know that you only have to write one "chunk" of the story at a time and this sequence of scenes must be in a predetermined length range. If you think it makes the writing process too simplistic, and by extension, easier than other literary forms, then be my guest and try it!

THE BENCHMARK 1-HOUR PILOT:

(INDUSTRY STANDARDS)

4-6 Acts total

(Teaser + 3-5 Acts)

54-58 pages

A, B, C story

THE BEAT SHEET

THE "FULL" STORY MAP

The Full Story Map adds a description of your main stories (the A, B, C and D stories) and the Beat Sheet, which is a list of plot points in your narrative. What happens from beginning to end in your pilot.

As said, you should have at least two stories, or lines of action, in your pilot—an "A" and "B" story. I like to refer to each individual story as a "story engine," as it is the dramatic construct that drives the action forward like an engine propels a car. A story engine must contain these three elements: A character, a goal, and the conflict standing in the way of the goal.

It's up to you how many stories to incorporate. *True Detective* has only an A and B story. *Scandal* uses an A, B, C and D story. Ideally, each story has at least three beats: a beginning, middle and end.

In your Story Map, it's best to keep your description of each engine short; not only does it make the map more readable but it helps you to focus each story.

Here are the four engines of the *Scandal* pilot:

A Story: Proving Lt. Colonel Sullivan's innocence.

B Story: Quinn's first day on the job.

C Story: President Grant and his intern.

D Story: Stephen's marriage proposal.

And the four engines of the *Game of Thrones* pilot:

A Story: Ned's offer from the King.

B Story: Daenerys marries Kal Drogo.

C Story: Jon Snow's place in the family.

D Story: Jaime and Cersei's relationship.

None of these stories can be an easy ride. Make sure you build contrast and conflict into each one. Never forget...

Drama = Conflict!

THE BEAT SHEET

If you study enough pilots, you will see that each act contains unmistakable characteristics. I've compiled the major characteristics below in a workable order, however, you must keep in mind that you will encounter variation from show to show. As you saw in "TV Script Lengths," every show has its own way of breaking down an episode into a multi-act structure – not every show uses the "Teaser plus five" act structure detailed below, so you must be flexible when it comes to overlapping of characteristics and beats.

For example, the beat I call the "Shadow Showdown" occurs in Act Four in *Scandal*, whereas in *True Detective* it occurs in Act Three. But that makes sense because there are more acts in *Scandal* (5) than in *True Detective* (4). But *The Walking Dead's* act structure is actually closer to *Scandal* than *True Detective*, and yet its Shadow Showdown occurs in Act Three. What gives?

Consider that the total running times of the shows differ, as each aired on a different network in its own unique time block of programming. (E.g., *The Walking Dead* is normally a one-hour show, but it was given an extended time slot for its premiere, thus the 66-minute running time of the pilot.) If you look at where the Shadow Showdown falls in each pilot, relative to the total number of pages/minutes, it's in the same basic zone. In *Scandal*, *True Detective* and *The Walking Dead*, it falls approximately 4/5ths of the way into the script.

You might think it wiser to give the relative locations of the beats – e.g., to say a beat falls *4/5ths of the way into your pilot* rather than *page 45 in Act Four* since it could very well fall in Act Three...but I'd rather get more specific with it. My aim is always to specify my beat sheets in more detail than others you might find. I'd rather give you a more specific template broken into specific page ranges than a rough approximation, until you get your sea legs and become proficient with this new form and format and you're able to experiment with structure.

With that said, you must know that <u>this not an exact science</u>. It cannot perfectly fit every one-hour television pilot. You may find a show that subverts this structure in some ways (*Game of Thrones* with its multi-protagonist structure comes to mind), or you may discover variation on the ordering of these "signpost" beats. Even so, I stand by this template as the best structural roadmap you will find, to date.

In the Beat Sheet breakdown below, I cite examples from *The Walking Dead*, *House of Cards* and *Breaking Bad* (complete beat sheets for each of these pilots can be found in **Case Studies**, along with *Scandal, Mr. Robot, True Detective, Game of Thrones and Mad Men.*)

Let's begin with the first section, often referred to as The Teaser.

TEASER (2-10 pages)

The Teaser is the launchpad for your story. It must suck us in and give us a strong reason to keep watching/reading. It begins with a compelling **Opening Sequence**. The Opening Sequence may constitute the whole of The Teaser or just one or two scenes in a larger section.

The Opening Sequence must contain **dynamic images**, a strong **sense of place**, **time** and **tone**, and an expression of the central **theme** of the series. Ideally, there is **movement** of some kind to inject a sense of energy and forward propulsion into the narrative, leading to a surprising **discovery**. Think about these memorable opening sequences:

In *The Good Wife*, we open on the image of a husband and wife's hands joined. In a tracking shot, we follow their hands as they enter a room filled with news photographers. Their hands separate as flash-bulbs explode, leading us to a press conference where the husband, a politician, defends allegations of impropriety and the wife bristles at the thought of his affair. This sequence ends with the wife slapping the husband and walking away from him, into her own, uncertain future.

In *Downton Abbey*, we follow the servants of the manor in an unbroken Steadicam shot. As they do their jobs, we see the opulent rooms of the mansion, perfectly establishing the time period and aristocratic tone. Meanwhile, we cross-cut to a teletype machine receiving a dramatic message and the morning paper spreading the news throughout the house. We will soon find out that *The Titanic* has just sunk, killing the rightful heir to the Abbey.

The pilot script for *Breaking Bad* (written by Vince Gilligan) opens on a character referred to as "Underwear Man" as he drives an RV like a bat out of hell, while wearing a gas mask.

Who the hell is this guy and what's going on?!

Below are more key characteristics of the Teaser, using *The Walking Dead, House of Cards* and *Breaking Bad* as examples. Try to incorporate as many of these characteristics into your Teaser as possible, at least three. And try to show them in a visual, or "active" way, as opposed to a character telling us all of this information in dialogue (Show, don't tell!). Everything does not need to be clear to the reader at this time, but keep in mind that the sooner you establish a line of action that moves forward (a character pursuing a goal against obstacles) the better.

- **Introduce a Fascinating Protagonist (Protag):** Show us who we will be following for 100 hours, in an active, unique way that says something about this person and their current, or soon-to-be, place in the world.
  The Walking Dead – Sheriff's Deputy Rick Grimes must make the terrible choice to kill a child / *House of Cards* – Senator Francis "Frank" Underwood mercy-kills a dog / *Breaking Bad* – Walter White, a schlub in his tighty-whities, crashes an RV in the desert.

- **Establish a Framing Device:** Establish how this story will be told, the glue that holds it together.
  TWD – Rick navigating a dystopian world / *HOC* – Frank narrates his schemes / *BB* – Open on a flash-forward of Walter in a crisis.

- **Express Theme**: Show us why you're writing this story, what it is about, in action. May be just a hint.
  TWD – Maintaining one's humanity in the apocalypse / *HOC* – Ambition / *BB* – Desperation.

- **Discover the "World:"** Give us at least a glimpse of your main setting, time period, milieu and the tone of this locale.
  TWD – Barren dystopia / *HOC* – Politicians in Washington, D.C. / *BB* – Life or death in the desert (as far as we know at this point).

- **Hint at Central Conflict ("The Compelling Crisis"):** Give us a taste of the ongoing dramatic dilemma of this series.
  TWD – Rick vs. zombies / *HOC* – Frank's relentless climb to the top / *BB* – Walter as a "fish out of water" in a criminal world.

- **CATALYST:** An event or reveal raises the stakes, defining the character in their current world and kicking a basic dramatic scenario into motion...

CATALYST (Teaser Act-Out):

	**The Walking Dead**: Rick shoots a little girl after discovering she is a zombie.
	**House of Cards:** Frank introduces us to his allies, the President-Elect and Chief of Staff. He has launched the first step of his grand plan.
	**Breaking Bad**: Walt records a video confession for his family, aims a gun in the direction of approaching sirens.

- **End on a Cliffhanger:** The Catalyst should leave us with an intense need to turn the page, a compelling hint at more to come. The launch of a fascinating dramatic question.

  TWD – How many more zombies are there?

  HOC – What is Frank's plan?

  BB – How did Walt get here and will he shoot the cops?

ACT ONE (12-15 pages):

Act One is often, but not always, the longest act in the pilot. It pushes the protagonist into action to confront the Compelling Crisis in a new world filled with friends and foes. Key characters drive new subplots. A "New Arrival" often tours the landscape, motivating crucial exposition. The "A" story, which is most often the protagonist's pursuit of their External Goal, must be established, and ideally, one or two other stories, as well, if not more. The order in which each story is launched is up to you. Stories are generally lettered by the writer according to screen time. I.e., the "A" story has the most screen time and the "D" story has the least. (These letter labels should never appear in your pilot script, by the way; they are for your use, only.)

Any major characteristics (your Basic Story Map elements) not covered in the Teaser should be included in Act One. For example, if your Teaser does not clearly express your theme, make sure to do it here. Perhaps more than any other act, Act One should be able to operate as its own closed story, with a beginning, middle and end, albeit with a cliffhanger at the end.

This cliffhanger, or "Act-Out," must be a shocking yet inevitable turn in direction that puts us on the edge of our seat and makes us turn the page. It is the "a-ha" moment that really illustrates where this story is going and solidifies your voice as the storyteller.

- **"A" Story:** Protagonist's central, external pursuit: *TWD* – Rick's struggle to survive in the new world / *House of Cards* – Frank's power play / *Breaking Bad* – Walt's meth business.

- **"B" Story:** A secondary, yet crucial, line of action that relates to a key dramatic element, such as...this story's mythology...a dynamic ally...the love interest...a hint at the full season arc... the Protag's "ghost" (backstory) or fatal flaw: *TWD* – Morgan and his wife / *HOC* – Zoe Barnes / *BB* – Walt's family.

- **"C" Story**: Key supporting characters in action: *TWD* – Rick and Shane / *HOC* – Peter Russo / *BB* – Hank.

- **"D" Story**: Supplementary line of action that helps to flesh out a character or the world: *TWD* – None. / *HOC* – Claire's non-profit. / *BB* – None.

- **New Arrival**: "Newborn" who arrives ignorant of the world: *TWD* – Rick / *HOC* – Zoe Barnes / *BB* – Walt.

- **Shadow Character** (may be same as New Arrival or Dynamic Ally): The opposite of the Protag: *TWD* – Morgan / *HOC* – Zoe Barnes / *BB* – Jesse Pinkman.

- **Dynamic Ally:** A key helper of the Protag: *TWD* – Morgan / *HOC* – Peter Russo / *BB* – Hank.

- **Theme:** The central idea being explored is cemented and integrated into Protag's goals: *TWD* – Humanity in the wake of disaster / *HOC* – Ambition / *BB* – Desperation.

- **Escalating Conflict/Stakes:** Complications arise: *TWD* – Rick and Shane set up roadblock, exchange fire with criminals / *HOC* – Workplace conflicts for all main characters / *BB* – Walt is humiliated at the car wash.

- **INCITING INCIDENT:** A surprising event of high conflict upsets the established order and stops the Protagonist in their tracks, while opening the door for a new journey, either setting the "A" story in motion, or, if it's already begun, accelerating it forward with new urgency...

INCITING INCIDENT:

	**The Walking Dead**: Rick is shot, blacks out, wakes up in the hospital, alone.*
	**House of Cards:** Frank is passed over for Secretary of State.
	**Breaking Bad**: At his 50th surprise birthday party, Walt is fascinated by Hank's seizure of $700k in drug money.*

TURN/Roadblock/Crisis to "A" and/or "B" story (Act One Act-Out):

A final surprising escalation of stakes that turns the story in a new direction and pushes the protagonist into the next stage, offering a cliffhanger or hint at more to come: *TWD* – Rick encounters his first pack of zombies *HOC* – Frank and wife Claire reconcile and team up / *BB* – Walt collapses.

*In pilots that employ flash-forwards in the Teaser, like *The Walking Dead* and *Breaking Bad*, we open the pilot with the "A" story already in motion, so it may not seem like the Inciting Incident launches the central line of action. But notice how the Inciting Incident in these two instances goes back to the start of the linear chronology to show us the beginning of the "A" line. Rick would not have encountered the zombie girl on his own if he had not been shot and left alone in the hospital, and Walt would not have crashed his RV had he not seen Hank's drug money and been inspired to start his own meth business as a way to raise money to fix his personal problems. Thus, these Inciting Incidents are truly the jumpstarting of their new journeys.

ACT TWO
(6-10 pages, often ends near page 30)

Act Two employs a strong escalation of conflict to turn the screws on our hero. It often comes with a location change, and it begins by showing us the result of the dramatic turn that came at the end of Act One. The protagonist usually gets themselves out of this predicament by making an active decision that will have dramatic consequences later, followed by more complications and inevitable crossing of paths with key characters.

The protagonist is thrown into a meaningful skirmish (First Trial) that produces some kind of failure or victim (First Casualty), which can be themselves, another character or a figurative death, like a loss of innocence. A significant event and/or decision of high conflict (Midpoint) signals a turn in direction for the story and raises the stakes, clarifying the Protag's "A" goal, ideally with a clear deadline (a "ticking time clock"). This beat creates a new challenge that propels them into the next Act and will pay off in the Climax of the pilot.

- **Aftermath of Cliffhanger**: The consequences of the previous Act-Out and/or a "taking stock" of the current dramatic situation. Vital exposition is given, setting up the engine of Act Two. Must involve an escalation of conflict, ideally followed by a decision/action by Protag that propels them toward their First Trial: *TWD* – Rick escapes the pack of zombies at the hospital, but when confronted by a slithering zombie torso, he runs / *HOC* – Frank and Doug lay out a plan / *BB* – Walt is told he has inoperable lung cancer; he keeps it a secret from his wife.

- **FIRST TRIAL/FIRST CASUALTY:** A skirmish between the protagonist and another character or antagonistic force results in a failure, loss or victim: *TWD* – Rick finds his home empty; he gets knocked out by Morgan / *HOC* – Frank clashes with wife Claire* / *BB* – Walt observes the drug bust, sees his former student Jesse escape.
House of Cards is the rare exception where the FT/FC occurs in Act One.

- **New complications to A, B, C stories:** More obstacles and threats are thrown at Protag and other key characters in more than one storyline: *TWD* – Rick is held captive by Morgan / *HOC* – Zoe's path collides with Frank's / *BB* – Walt learns about money problems from his wife and blows up at his boss at the car wash.

- **MIDPOINT "A" Story:** At the halfway point, a major event or decision TURNS the direction of (at least) the "A" story, ups the stakes, clarifies or alters Protag's goal and launches a line of action that will push to the climax, ideally with an urgent "ticking time clock." Often forces Protag to make a decision. Raises a new dramatic question, even if not explicitly stated. There must be a connection between the Midpoint and the ending...

MIDPOINT (Act Two Act-Out):

	**The Walking Dead**: Rick is told about the "Walkers" and sees Morgan's undead wife.
	**House of Cards:** Frank takes the job to draft the education bill with his arch-rival, Kern.
	**Breaking Bad**: Walt blackmails Jesse into partnering with him in the meth trade.

- **New Question/Challenge...** *TWD* – Will Rick have the strength to kill his family, if they have become Walkers, just as Morgan must kill his wife? / *HOC* – How will Frank use the education bill to defeat Kern? / *BB* – Can Walt and Jesse work together in their own meth business?

ACT THREE (8-12 pages, ends around page 40)

Act Three finds various lines of action intersecting, which escalate conflict and force a dramatic confrontation between our protagonist and their Shadow (Shadow Showdown), and interweave and overlap stories so the protagonist and their Dynamic Ally are now working together or perhaps even at odds.

The protagonist makes an important decision that is often a character-defining action. This "Assumption of Power" moment is a show of strength as they fully commit ("Going All In"), honoring their own personal code and taking control. The order of these beats may differ from show to show, but notice how the AOP beat falls in the range of 37-40 in most of our sample pilots in **Case Studies**.

- **Aftermath of Midpoint:** The consequences of the Midpoint Turn/Decision and how Protag deals with the higher stakes. They should be moving forward, not just taking stock: *TWD* – Rick returns to his home, confirms his belief that his family is alive / *HOC* – Frank tells Doug to set up a meeting with Catherine Durant / *BB* - Walt steals chemistry equipment from his school.

- **SHADOW SHOWDOWN:** Direct confrontation/paralleling between Protag and their Shadow: *TWD* – Rick and Morgan both attempt mercy killings. Only Rick has the strength to pull the trigger / *HOC* – Zoe and Frank face off, finding common ground, but he rebuffs her / *BB* – Walt and Jesse fight over their opposing scientific methods.

- **Partial Integration of lines** (A-B, B-C, etc.): Crossover between stories as Protag interacts with major supporting characters: *TWD* – Rick learns from Morgan that there may be a large survivor colony outside town / *HOC* – Frank recruits Zoe / *BB* – Walt steals chemistry equipment.

- **ASSUMPTION OF POWER:** Protagonist takes full control and shows their strength in a successful strike. A bold move, as they "go all in"...

ASSUMPTION OF POWER (Act Three Act-Out):

	**The Walking Dead**: Rick raids the weapons closet at the police station.
	**House of Cards:** Frank shreds the education bill and passes it to Zoe.
	**Breaking Bad**: Walt empties his savings to buy an RV to act as their lab, and roughs up a bully mocking his son.

ACT FOUR (6-12 pages, ends around page 48)

Act Four takes us outside of our central throughline to visit supporting characters as they deal with their own personal conflicts, advancing and/or ending the B, C and D stories. Meanwhile, the protagonist must deal with the consequences of decisions they've made in Acts Two and Three, take decisive action (Declaration of War), essentially delivering on promises and finally doing what they were meant to do (e.g., Rick becomes an old west-style sheriff, Frank recruits Zoe for his final plan, and Walt cooks pure meth.).

But their accomplishments don't last long, as this movement culminates in their highest stakes, most vulnerable moment yet and they hit bottom (All is Lost). Alternatively, the protagonist may get a big win, but it still must raise the stakes or create a new challenge of some kind.

- **Skirmishes and Complications:** Protag and others take steps toward their goals, hit obstacles, make shocking discoveries, all serving to up the stakes and pay off earlier setups. *TWD* – Rick runs out of gas / *HOC* – Frank tests Zoe / *BB* – Walt struggles to train Jesse in correct chemistry; Jesse gets into trouble with his former partner and Krazy-8, a local dealer.

- **Integration, Escalation, Stopping Points:** Crossover of stories escalate conflict and create crisis moments for Protag and supporting characters. Events occur that will have ramifications beyond the pilot. B, C and D stories may come to an end. *TWD* – Shane is now with Rick's wife / *HOC* – Zoe hands in her story and Frank blackmails Peter / *BB* – Jesse brings the dealers to Walt, and they recognize him from Hank's DEA sting.

- **DECLARATION OF WAR & ALL IS LOST**: If the Assumption of Power was a show of strength, the DOW* is a full-on assault, and the Protagonist formulates the specific "method of defeat" by which they will overcome the antagonistic forces keeping them from their goal. This is usually a **Big Risk** that seems to signal a **Big Win,** but it is a false victory, leading to a hitting bottom **"All is Lost"** dilemma...

DOW & ALL IS LOST (Act Four Act-Out):

	**The Walking Dead**: Rick mounts a horse, rides into town, but soon gets surrounded by hungry Walkers.
	**House of Cards:** Frank leaks the education bill to Zoe, but Linda Vasquez puts his plan in jeopardy.
	**Breaking Bad**: Rival drug dealers hold Walt at gunpoint. He postpones his death by teaching them his recipe in the RV.

*The DOW can also fall in Act Five, but usually occurs about 4/5ths of the way into the pilot.

ACT FIVE (2-8 pages, The Final Clash):

Act Five brings the A story to a surprising climax and resolution, and advances the other stories (if they're still going) to a stopping point that promises more to come. This final movement may take the form of a short epilogue tying up loose threads, as with the two scenes in *Mad Men*'s final act (which features a final reveal that I like to call a BIG ENDING), or a larger, more active sequence like *Breaking Bad*'s fight with the drug dealers.

Whatever the case, it must be shocking yet feel organic while being consistent with theme, and it must show dramatic <u>change</u> from the opening sequence of the pilot.

In the end, the protagonist has crossed the portal into a new world and we can't wait to continue the journey with them.

- **CLIMAX (A, B)**: The final battle, ideally a direct confrontation, leads to success, or, at least, a temporary resolution, for the Protagonist. *TWD* – Rick barely escapes a huge mob of Walkers / *HOC* – Zoe publishes cover story about the education bill, as per Frank's plan / *BB* – Walt takes out Krazy-8, evades the law and launders his money (literally!).

- **EPILOGUE/ THE NEW WORLD**: The new status of our Protagonist in their changed world, with a hint of more to come...

EPILOGUE:

	**The Walking Dead**: Rick is pinned down in a tank, surrounded by hundreds of Walkers, as he hears a voice on the radio.
	**House of Cards**: Frank's plan comes together as the education bill story ruins Kern and promotes Zoe, and he enjoys VIP seating at the inauguration.
	**Breaking Bad**: Walt, a new man, has passionate sex with his wife Skyler.

Finally, we are left with the feeling of an approaching storm, a...

HANGING QUESTION/CLIFFHANGER (END OF PILOT):

How will Rick escape alive?

What will Frank do with his access to the new President?

Will Walt tell his wife about his cancer and his new enterprise?

THE BENCHMARK 1-HOUR PILOT
(ACT STRUCTURE GUIDELINES)

Teaser (2-10 pages)

Act One (12-15 pages)

Act Two (6-10 pages, ends around page 30)

Act Three (8-12 pages, ends around page 40)

Act Four (6-12 pages, ends around page 48)

Act Five (2-8 pages)

CASE STUDIES: BEAT SHEETS FOR *SCANDAL, MR. ROBOT, TRUE DETECTIVE, THE WALKING DEAD, GAME OF THRONES, BREAKING BAD, HOUSE OF CARDS* AND *MAD MEN*

The beat sheets below combine with their "Basic" Story Maps to create eight "Full" Story Maps. We already looked at an example of the Basic Story Map for *Scandal* (in **The TV Drama Story Map**).

Not all of the beat sheets below are complete scene lists; most have been trimmed to focus on the "signpost" beats that form the bones of the narrative.

All of these beat sheets have been made from the completed episodes, transcribed as I watched them, either on DVD or streaming. The numbers at the start of each beat represent the time in minutes the beat occurred, which correspond to the page numbers in a properly formatted script. Remember that one minute of screen time generally equates to one page of screenplay, so, for example, an Inciting Incident 11 minutes into the episode would roughly fall on page 11 of the script. However, if you were to read the actual scripts of our eight sample pilots, you may find differences from the aired episodes. This is because changes are inevitably made in the editing room—scenes are cut, trimmed, moved around, etc. But I still recommend you try to get your hands on some pilot scripts, as it is always an interesting exercise to make a script to screen comparison. Keep in mind, however, that it can be difficult for an outsider to confirm if a script was a shooting draft or an earlier work in progress.

Also, please know that if you see overlap in numbers, that means that a scene began within the same minute that the previous scene ended. Obviously, not every scene is going to time out to an exact minute.

SCANDAL PILOT
"SWEET BABY"

Written By Shonda Rhimes

Scandal is a great example of a major network drama. A strong female protagonist leads a dynamic ensemble in a hybrid procedural/serial format that incorporates a "case of the week" with longer arcs of story and character. The Compelling Crisis is familiar—a Washington, D.C. "fixer" is called in on various assignments as her own personal life spins out of control—but the execution is fresh, or, at least, top-notch. It's just gritty enough to work in ABC's 9 P.M. slot, but sans the nudity and violence of HBO fare.

Shonda Rhimes' script is an incredibly tight pilot that pretty much does everything right, and in only 45 minutes, making it the shortest of our sample pilots. It introduces every major character *in action* (even the two-person dialogue scene that opens the pilot is thrilling and suggestive of movement as our "Newborn" Quinn is offered a high-stakes job and told she has to decide in the moment). We see this high-stakes world in action in the very next scene as we meet Olivia Pope, our hero, standing up to gangsters and negotiating successfully for a mystery package, which in a great reveal is soon shown to be a baby. The Teaser ends with a man entering Olivia's office, bloody, saying he didn't kill his girlfriend. This is six minutes in and we've already launched the A, B and D story. As you can see below in the beat sheet, the pilot is front-loaded, with both Catalyst and Inciting Incident occurring in the six minute Teaser. Interestingly, in an early draft of the script, Sully enters on page 12. As with many effective rewrites, the Inciting Incident was moved up so as to get the story moving as soon as possible. In a pilot, the first few minutes cannot be more important—millions are watching and looking for reasons to turn the channel, maybe to never tune in again. The clock is ticking.

But a well-executed procedural is not enough to make it in today's fractured TV landscape. A new drama needs a *noisy* hook, and that's exactly what Shonda Rhimes injected into this story. What really makes this pilot shine is the "C" story, which begins as a case that sounds familiar and cliché: a sex scandal with the President of the United States and his intern. But although we get some effective scenes of Olivia investigating the case, the true turn in the "C" story occurs in Act Four and will have ramifications well beyond the pilot: Olivia and President Grant are former lovers...and he wants her back. This is a textbook "Shadow Showdown" beat.

I particularly like how the theme shifts and sharpens late in the episode with a deft mix of scene order, subtext, and dramatic mirroring – what was once a story about secrets and lies becomes a tale of true love.

Scandal may not be one of your go-to shows, but I urge you to watch the pilot. Watch and learn.

SCANDAL

Pilot "Sweet Baby" (2012)

Written by Shonda Rhimes / Directed by Paul McGuigan

TEASER

1-2 **OPENING ("B")**: In a bar, QUINN gets a surprise job interview by HARRISON to work for the famous Olivia Pope. They are not a legal firm. They are the good guys. Harrison makes Quinn repeat these words: "I want to be a gladiator in a suit." ("B" story: Quinn's first day on the job)

[QUICK TITLE: *Scandal*]

3-4 **CATALYST**: In a dark warehouse, OLIVIA POPE talks to her handsome employee STEPHEN about him proposing to his girlfriend ("D" story: Stephen's proposal). Olivia boldly transacts a shady business deal with Russian mobsters, convincing them to take half the money they asked for: $3 million. They back down, hand her the package and she leaves.

5-6 Back at Olivia's office, newbie Quinn meets the team. They all ignore her. Quinn watches in awe as Olivia hands the package off to her happy clients, the Russian Ambassador and his wife: it's their baby! She successfully negotiated with Russian gangsters to return their kidnapped baby to them.

6 **INCITING INCIDENT**: LT. COL. SULLIVAN "SULLY" ST. JAMES walks into the office, covered in blood. His girlfriend was just killed, and the police think he did it. ("A" story: Proving Sullivan's innocence) FADE OUT.

ACT ONE

7-10 **WORLD**: Sullivan's background and the "rules" of Olivia Pope's practice. Olivia narrates a montage that shows their process – Olivia always goes with her gut. Her one rule to Sully: "Don't lie."

Olivia and her TEAM go into action.

15-16 **TURN**: CYRUS comes to Olivia with a new job. Intern making sexual allegations against Fitzgerald Grant, the <u>President of the United States</u>. ("C" story: The President and his intern.). **DECISION**: Olivia demands to <u>look in his eyes</u>.

ACT TWO

16-17 **AFTERMATH**: Check-in with Stephen and his proposal. Abby is secretly in love with Stephen. Quinn finds key evidence, proving herself a **Dynamic Ally**.

18-19 **FIRST TRIAL**: At Camp David, Olivia and PRESIDENT FITZGERALD GRANT. He denies, she studies him...takes the case.

20 New evidence, care of Abby: Sully's deceased girlfriend Paige was having an affair. This presents an **"A" ROADBLOCK** as it points to motive for Sully to kill her.

20-21 **FIRST CASUALTY**: Quinn tags along with Olivia to the park. Olivia intimidates AMANDA TANNER, the President's intern. Quinn is troubled **("B" ROADBLOCK)**. Olivia walks away, makes a quick call, saying "It's handled." But is it?

ACT THREE

22-24 **AFTERMATH**: Quinn sobs in the bathroom, HUCK helps her. <u>No crying</u>—Olivia doesn't believe in it! ("Crying" setup)

24 Olivia still trying to get a bead on Grant. Questioning her gut.

MIDPOINT ("A" STORY): BOMBSHELL: Sully's prints are on the gun!

25-28 **COMPLICATIONS**: Sully comes clean — he knew about Paige's affair and he reveals that he picked up the gun after finding her body.

Olivia shows diamond engagement rings to Stephen. He chooses one. Olivia: "Good choice."

ROADBLOCK: Cops storm in to arrest Sully. Olivia negotiates with the head cop to give them 40 minutes. (<u>Ticking Time Clock</u>)

29-32 **TURN**: Sully <u>is gay</u>. But he will not come out, even though his alibi is that he was with his male lover at the time of the murder. "I'm a hero. I can't be gay." He is arrested.

IMPOSSIBLE CHOICES: For Sully, he can go to jail for a crime he didn't commit or ruin his honor and career. For Olivia, she can honor her client's wishes and lose his case or win his case and ruin his life.

Quinn reports that Amanda Tanner is in the hospital after a suicide attempt.

ALL IS LOST on the A, B and C lines.

ACT FOUR

33-34 **AFTERMATH**: Reviewing details of the case, "taking stock." Olivia hears "Sweet baby." She storms off.

35-38 **ASSUMPTION OF POWER & SHADOW SHOWDOWN**: Olivia confronts President Grant in the Oval Office. She knows he slept with Amanda, because Olivia used to be his "sweet baby!" He betrayed her trust, made her question her gut. She tries to resist his advances, but she can't and he kisses her. Cyrus catches them.

39-40 **INTEGRATION**: Still shaken from the Oval Office, Olivia watches Stephen propose to his girlfriend and she accepts. (End "D" story) Olivia cries ("Crying" payoff).

41-42 **DECLARATION OF WAR**: Olivia visits Sully in a jail cell in one last push to convince him to give her the name of his lover, to come clean and claim his alibi. (THEME SHIFTS: The episode is now about <u>true love</u>.) She is a mirror to Sully, in that they both have a secret love that jeopardizes their career and tears them up inside. She begs him to reveal the truth and we know that she's also trying to give herself the courage to admit to her love for the President.

ACT FIVE

42 **CLIMAX ("A")**: Sully admits he's gay in a press conference. He is acquitted of all charges. (End "A" story)

43-44 **EPILOGUE/NEW WORLD**: The team wraps up evidence for the police. Quinn is now a member of the team. **CLIMAX ("B")**: She says it and she means it: "Gladiators in suits." (End "B" story)

44-45 **CLIMAX ("C")**: Olivia delivers a bombshell to Cyrus: <u>Amanda Tanner just became her client</u>! She's taking on the President of the United States, her former lover. (End "C" story)

CLIFFHANGER: How can she win against the President? Has Sully given her the strength to reveal the truth to the world about her own affair?

MR. ROBOT PILOT
"eps1.0_hellofriend.mov"

Written By Sam Esmail

Mr. Robot was a sleeper hit in the summer of 2015, giving a nice jolt of energy to a stagnating USA Network slate with perfect timing in a year of high-profile corporate hacks. I must admit, I was reluctant to give it a chance, considering the horribly on the nose title. But after many friends recommended it, I discovered a fantastic pilot that utilizes the "Teaser plus five" Story Map in every crucial way. It takes a lot of familiar parts and weaves them together into an expertly paced whole that leaves us hooked to watch more.

The archetypes are nothing new. It's part *The Matrix*, part *Fight Club*, with an anti-social hacker vigilante hero (who is a drug addict, of course) we've seen too many times in the last two decades. There's a boardroom filled with a bunch of creepy rich guys in suits, a posse of menacing Men in Black, a mega-corporation known as "Evil Corp," and there's even a Ferris Wheel scene that some would say recalls *The Third Man*. Yet it feels fresh, because the details feel authentic as the story finds unique methods of turning the screws on our young, troubled protagonist. And it's the humanity of the characters we discover within this dark, digital world that really makes it come alive.

We care about Elliot from the first scene, when his monologue reveals crucial details about his character and his past, like his emotional isolation and his father's death due to company malfeasance. This talky teaser needed a big ending, and it comes in the form of the police arriving to arrest the kiddy porn trafficker. We believe Elliot when he says he doesn't care about money, and only an expert could have hacked the trafficker, thus making Elliot the perfect person for the mysterious Mr. Robot to recruit to erase the world's credit card debt. It's not until the extended Midpoint sequence that peaks in the E-Corp server farm that Elliot passes the first test that will make him Mr. Robot's next cyber-soldier, and it takes until Act Four for Robot's full plan of attack to be revealed. Still, Elliot's not convinced he wants to join this underground army, not until the one person that he truly cares about is wronged. It's E-Corp CEO Colby's act of banishing Angela from the cyber-security team that pushes Elliot to hand over Colby's IP address to the FBI just as Mr. Robot had instructed. This is Elliot's Declaration of War, his "Going All In" and "All Is Lost" moment.

This points out a key difference between Elliot and Mr. Robot, just one of the ways in which they make great Shadows of one another: Elliot acts locally and for personal reasons, whereas Robot acts in order to bring about a global revolution, not caring about collateral damage. The differences continue. According to him, Elliot's father was a good man killed by a corrupt system. Robot's father was a criminal that got caught, losing his son's respect in the process. Elliot is a lone wolf who faces his targets, while Robot works in anonymity with a team. Elliot works inside the machine and Robot is off the grid. These two have many conflicts ahead of them, yet they are bound by purpose.

Like all effective pilots, *Mr. Robot* lays a lot of track for future arcs. We are introduced to several characters with long-term potential. The E-Corp brass, Mr. Robot's hacker crew, Shayla the dealer/girlfriend, Krista the therapist, Angela the best friend, Gideon the AllSafe boss who trusts Elliott enough to reveal a personal secret. The psychological angle adds another fun layer to keep us guessing. We follow the story through Elliot's eyes and are privy to his thoughts via voiceover—can we trust what we are seeing when even he questions his reality?

The opening and closing images of the mysterious boardroom cabal are bookends, but when the group is ultimately revealed to be led by Tyrell Wellick, Elliott breaks the fourth wall and pleads with us in voiceover: "Please tell me you're seeing this, too."

MR. ROBOT

Pilot ""eps1.0_hellofriend.mov"" (2015)

Written by Sam Esmail / Directed by Niels Arden Oplev

TEASER

1 **OPENING**: V.O. from ELLIOT over images of shadowy men in a conference room. They are "the top 1% of the top 1%" who are secretly running the world. And he believes they're following him.

New York City. On a subway train, Elliot is being watched by men in dark suits.

2-7 **CATALYST**: At a coffee shop, Elliot meets with the OWNER. He shows him evidence of the child pornography he hacked from the man's private servers. The man thinks Elliot wants money, but Elliot's intentions are for justice; the police arrive to take the man into custody and Elliot walks away.

ACT ONE

7 A DRUNK (whom we will meet later) on the subway speaks to Elliot, tells him it's "an exciting time in the world right now." Elliot ignores him.

8 Elliot reports to his job at Allsafe cyber-security firm, where his boss GIDEON is angry that their client is still getting hacked. ("A" Story: Elliot, Mr. Robot and E-Corp) Elliot's best friend from childhood, ANGELA, 20s, a junior account exec, got him the job here. ("C" Story: Elliot and Angela)

9 Angela is upset that Elliot didn't attend her birthday party at a bar the night before. Flash to Elliot standing outside the bar, scared. He has social phobia, and doesn't like being touched.

10 Elliot can't stand Angela's boyfriend, OLLIE. Ollie can't understand why Elliot doesn't like him.

11-15 Elliot talks to his therapist KRISTA. ("B" Story: Krista and her boyfriend) He doesn't tell her that he did some hacking and found out she's dating a guy named Michael Hansen with no internet footprint, which makes Elliot suspicious. Elliot gives a passionate monologue about why he hates society, but it turns out to be in his head; he never said it aloud. When Krista asks him if he's still seeing the "men in black," he lies to her and says no.

15-17 At Allsafe, Ollie asks Elliot to lunch, but Elliot says no. Elliot hacked Ollie and knows he's cheating on Angela.

18-19 **INCITING INCIDENT**: The execs from their biggest client, E-CORP, arrive. Elliot calls them "Evil Corp." TERRY COLBY, the CTO, is a douche with a Blackberry, but his younger right-hand man TYRELL WELLICK seems to genuinely be tech-savvy. **TURN**: Tyrell seems to be fascinated by Elliot. But why?

20-21 Elliot comes home to a drab, empty apartment. His only company is his fish "Qwerty." Later, Elliot cries, then he snorts a measured amount of morphine. His sexy drug dealer, SHAYLA, comes over to deliver some pills. She offers him ecstasy.

ACT TWO

22-24 **AFTERMATH**: Elliot lies awake in bed with a naked Shayla sleeping next to him. He goes out alone to the streets to do some work. **FIRST TRIAL/FIRST CASUALTY**: Elliot tracks Michael Hansen and Krista on a date. He tricks Michael into giving him his cell phone number, so he can hack him. He notices Michael is mean to his little dog, "Flipper." (Dog setup)

25-30 **MIDPOINT:** Angela calls Elliot from work because E-Corp has just suffered a massive hack. He comes in to try to stop the quickly spreading virus, but he can't do it from the office. Gideon flies him to E-Corp's HQ so he can work in E-Corp's server farm. Elliot saves the day with some brilliant coding.

30 **TURN**: The anonymous hackers left a signature, "fsociety," with the message "LEAVE ME HERE."

31 **DECISION**: Elliot leaves the malicious code in the E-Corp mainframe and reconfigures it so only he has access to the server.

ACT THREE

32 **AFTERMATH**: On the corporate jet home, Gideon shares a secret with Elliot: he's gay. Gideon says that he can talk to Elliot, more than the others. Gideon is worried that they might lose E-Corp as a client, which is 80% of their business. Elliot promises him that he will find the hackers.

35-40 **SHADOW SHOWDOWN**: On the subway, the drunk reveals himself as "MR. ROBOT," the one who put the root virus code on the E-Corp server. He tells Elliot a story about his father, a petty thief who lost his respect when he got caught and went to jail. Mr. Robot takes Elliot to his secret tech room in Coney Island, introducing him to his team of eccentric TECHIES. Elliot is scared to join them.

ACT FOUR

41-42 Angela shows up at Elliot's apartment for a movie night. She sees Shayla still in Elliot's bed and says she's happy that he's "dating." He is embarrassed.

42-48 **ASSUMPTION OF POWER**: Elliot gathers evidence online, making up a file to give to the police to turn in "fsociety." On the Ferris Wheel on Coney Island, Mr. Robot pitches Elliot his grand scheme to erase all of E-Corp's files, and, by extension, all of the debt owed to them by the common man. He calls it the biggest incident of wealth redistribution in history. Their first target will be Terry Colby. Elliot must give the FBI Colby's IP address so it looks like he did the hack, and it will set in motion a revolution. Elliot does not agree to do it.

Elliot researches debt, disparity of wealth, and makes up one of his data CDs, unsure if he will use it.

50-54 **INTEGRATION (A & C)**: Elliot sits in a big meeting at Allsafe led by Terry Colby. When Angela makes one small mistake, Terry has her unceremoniously removed from the room, shocking Elliot.
DECLARATION OF WAR: Elliot gives the FBI the report with Colby's IP address. (Elliot goes **"ALL IN"** and **"ALL IS LOST."**)

ACT FIVE

55 **AFTERMATH**: It's been 19 days and nothing has happened. Elliot turns to Krista's deadbeat boyfriend, Michael.

56-58 **CLIMAX ("B")**: Elliot blackmails Michael, demanding that he break up with Krista, tonight, *and* come clean to her about his wife and affairs. Elliot also takes Flipper. (Dog payoff) (End "B" Story)

60 **CLIMAX ("C")**: Elliot confronts Angela, who's been avoiding him. She tells him not to stick up for her like he did in the meeting, says "Let me lose." He hugs her, maybe for the first time, and they share a moment. (End "C" Story)

62 **CLIMAX ("A")**: Terry Colby has been arrested! Mr. Robot's plan worked. But Elliot's celebration is cut short when he is thrown into a car by MEN IN BLACK.

64 **EPILOGUE**: Elliot is brought to the conference room where the group of BUSINESS MEN in suits gather (the 1% of the 1% glimpsed in the Opening montage). Their leader is <u>Tyrell Wellick</u>. Elliot turns to us.

>   ELLIOT (V.O.)
>   Please tell me you're seeing
>   this, too.

TRUE DETECTIVE PILOT
"THE LONG BRIGHT DARK"

Written By Nic Pizzolatto

In early 2013, the television landscape was rocked by the debut of *True Detective*, an epic 8-episode drama from HBO that blurred the line between television and cinema more than ever. It was a serial killer crime procedural -- as familiar a genre as they come -- but the execution was so unique and at such a high level of craft that the series immediately established itself with viewers and critics alike as one of the great achievements in the modern era of television drama.

From the start, the series broke with convention. One writer, one director, for all eight episodes. Two big movie stars in the lead roles. Three separate time periods, spanning 17 years. A focus on character over plot, with a "literary" (to borrow a term from the original pitch document) approach that incorporated complex philosophical theories with multiple story threads and a rich off-screen world. Episodes would often end on an ambiguous note, with a teasing element left merely in subtext. In fact, key elements were often introduced, not to pop up again for another two or three episodes. There was a trust in the audience that they would not only watch closely but analyze the content, discuss it online and wait for the convergence of all of these threads in a slam-bang climax.

With the long time frame and the extensive cross-cutting between 1995 and 2012, narrative structure in *True Detective* was a huge undertaking. The pilot episode, "The Long Bright Dark," needed to clearly establish the framing device of the 2012 interviews with the seamless interweaving of the 1995 murder investigation (while hinting at events in 2002, a third time period to come), show the theme in action with the defining characteristics of our two leads as they drove the story forward, drop a few details of the sprawling criminal case while teasing others, and fit it all into a tight five act structure with cliffhanger endings for each act. I should note that my original map was only four acts in total, but I chose to define a short Act Four as a "bridge act" since this section feels like a separate movement, followed by a slightly longer Act Five. I suggest you watch the episode with the map in front of you, as it is quite complex.

We will not discuss season two of *True Detective*. It's best left alone.

TRUE DETECTIVE

Pilot "The Long Bright Dark" (2014)

Written by Nic Pizzolatto / Directed by Cary Fukunaga

ACT ONE

1 [OPENING TITLES SEQUENCE]

2-4 **FRAMING DEVICE (Interviews in 2012)** established as we watch two men being interviewed by the same duo of police officers ("A" story: Hart and Cohle's partnership):

MARTIN HART (**Rustin's Dynamic Ally and Shadow**) talks about his former partner, Rustin Cohle, who was known as an odd sort, from Texas; they called him the "Tax Man." They'd only worked together for four months before they caught the case of Dora Lange and the kids in the woods, in 1995.

RUSTIN COHLE looks worse for wear. Refuses to stop smoking in the interview room. They caught the case on January 3, 1995, his daughter's birthday...

5-8 **INCITING INCIDENT (1995)**: Cohle and Hart show up to the crime scene, the ritualistic slaying of a young woman. Naked corpse is tied to a tree, wearing antlers, with tattoos, possibly Satanic. Cohle takes meticulous notes and makes drawings in his big ledger, which is how he got the nickname Tax Man. ("B" story: The Dora Lange murder.)

(2012) Back to the interviews, Hart expounds on the different kinds of cops (**THEME**: What makes a "true detective"). Cohle was very smart, quiet, but "past a certain age, a man without a family can be a bad thing." Cohle lives alone in a tiny bare apartment, sleeps on a mattress on the floor, surrounded by stacks of books on serial killers and police work.

10 (1995) Cohle studies sculptures left at the crime scene: bundles of

sticks tied together in a triangular pattern, hanging from the tree. He comes up with a theory on the killer, a "metapsychotic" who will kill again. Hart thinks Cohle is jumping to conclusions, warns against bending the narrative to support an assumption.

12 Hart awkwardly invites Cohle to his home for dinner. Hart's wife has been insisting on the invitation.

14 **TURN**: Cohle shows up at Hart's house that night, drunk. **COMPELLING CRISIS:** The "family man" forced to team up with the "unstable single guy."

ACT TWO

14-18 **AFTERMATH**: In the car after the crime scene, Hart and Cohle clash over religion and the nature of humanity. Hart regrets his attempt to get Cohle to open up.

18-21 At police HQ, Hart vouches for Cohle to his CAPTAIN. Hart will remain the lead on the case, and lead a debriefing at a press conference tomorrow.

22-26 **FIRST TRIAL**: Cohle on his own at night, questioning hookers about the victim. Cohle asks a PROSTITUTE to get him pills so he can sleep. **FIRST CASUALTY**: Cole is a mess, possibly a drug addict.

28 **MIDPOINT**: The victim is ID'd: Dora Kelly Lange, a former prostitute (as Cohle predicted and Hart doubted).

30-34 **NEW COMPLICATIONS:** They find no evidence at the morgue. They argue again. Cohle tells Hart, "I don't sleep, I just dream." They are told about a little girl that went missing years ago named Marie Fonteneau. (Setup for later episodes: the first victim.)

34-35 **TURN**: At a black church, Cohle shows his ledger to the PASTOR, who recognizes the stick sculptures. **HINT AT MORE/NEW CHALLENGE**: His grandma used to call them "Devil's Nets." Occult items.

ACT THREE

35-36 AFTERMATH (1995): They talk to SHERIFF TATE, a pompous ass, about the Fonteneau case and another girl who was chased through the forest by a man she called the "green-eared spaghetti monster." (Setup for later episodes: the killer's facial scars.)

38 Hart and Cohle talk to Dora Lange's ex-husband CHARLIE in jail. The last time he saw her, she was high and talking nonsense, like she "met a King." (Setup for later episodes: the killer known as the "Yellow King.")

40 ASSUMPTION OF POWER ("B") (2012): Cohle surprises the cops when he tells them he knows that they're on the case of the recent murder in Lake Charles.

41-47 SHADOW SHOWDOWN (1995): Dinner at Hart's home with his wife MAGGIE and two young girls. Hart takes pity on drunk Cohle and offers to create a reason for him to duck out after ten minutes. At the dinner table, Cohle reveals to Maggie that he had a daughter that died, which led to the breakup of his marriage. Hart gives Cohle the opportunity to leave as they had planned, but Cohle stays. Hart steams.

48 ASSUMPTION OF POWER ("A") (2012): Hart reveals that he stopped talking to Cohle in 2002. The reasons for their falling-out were private, not related to the Dora Lange case. (Setup for later episodes: the incident that led to their breakup.) Even so, he makes it clear to the detectives that Cohle was a good cop.

ACT FOUR

49-50 DECLARATION OF WAR (1995): In the HQ, Cohle hits a fellow cop, showing no fear. The others think Cohle's a former Internal Affairs rat.

50-52 INTEGRATION ("A" & "B"): The cops meet REVEREND TUTTLE, who mentions the creation of a special division to focus on anti-Christian crimes, angering Cohle. **ALL IS LOST:** Hart tells Cohle that he pissed off the wrong guy—Tuttle is first cousin of Louisiana Governor Tuttle! Hart warns Cohle to watch his ass, as powerful people are now tracking them.

ACT FIVE

53 Cohle and Hart visit Marie Fonteneau's AUNT and UNCLE, who looked after Marie when her parents dropped out of the picture.

56 **CLIMAX "B" STORY (1995)**: Cohle finds a discovery in the shed: a Devil's Net! The Aunt claims she's never seen it before.

57 **CLIMAX "A" STORY (2012)**: Cohle gets the cops to show him a photo of the Lake Charles murder scene: a blonde woman is strung up naked under a bridge with antlers on her head. Almost identical to the 1995 crime scene.

58 **CLIFFHANGER (2012)**: Cohle asks the big hanging question:

```
          COHLE
     How could this murder be the work
     of the same killer when we caught
     him back in 1995?
```

THE WALKING DEAD PILOT
"DAYS GONE BYE"

Written By Frank Darabont

In 2010, AMC sent me an advance screener for a new show titled *The Walking Dead*. As I read the promotional materials, my first thought was, *Wow, no one's ever done zombies on TV before. Clever idea*. Then I watched the pilot, "Days Gone Bye," written and directed by Frank Darabont of *Shawshank Redemption* fame, and I found myself saying aloud, "This is going to be HUGE." It was just so fresh, so well-executed.

Cut to today and *The Walking Dead* is the highest rated show on television, and the first scripted show since 2007 to defeat live NFL football in the U.S. overnight ratings. In our age of time-shifted DVR viewing and torrenting, this level of "appointment viewing" is, well, huge.

But it wasn't just the novelty of a TV series in a fresh genre that sucked in viewers from the get-go, it was the treatment of the material -- the dramatic decisions made by Darabont as to how to reveal information, story engines and characters in the crucial first hour of what was designed as a sprawling saga.

Watching the pilot after several years, the biggest thing that jumps out at me is that there are two major characters in the pilot, a father and son, MORGAN and DUANE, who do not appear in the rest of the season. (Morgan doesn't even pop up again until season three.) So why get the audience invested in these characters, only to drop them? There's a number of reasons, all revealed by the Full Story Map.

Firstly, Morgan and Duane are vehicles to deliver vital exposition, to inform our protagonist and us about the "rules" of this new world. Secondly, they add the "B" story to the pilot, which is especially crucial here as the protagonist, Sheriff Rick Grimes, is in almost every scene so we needed a break from that line of action (the "A" story, Rick navigating the new world and learning when to kill and when to hold fire). Thirdly, since Rick's closest loved ones are separated from him and not given much screen time (the "C" story of the survivor colony), Morgan and Duane stand in for them, providing an active emotional throughline that we can all relate to. As Rick is our way into the external line of man vs. zombies, Morgan and Duane are our way into the internal line of the destructive family dynamics caused by this dystopian world.

Notice also how each act brings a new movement, a distinct engine, and each movement comes to a clear end by the end of the act, with a hint of more that makes us sit through the commercial break.

I particularly like the "Shadow Showdown" in Act Three: a powerful montage in which Rick and Morgan must commit separate acts of mercy, putting zombie victims out of their misery. Rick apologizes to his victim, a nameless zombie missing her lower half, before he pulls the trigger. In Morgan's case, his target is not so simple: the zombie is his wife and Duane's mother. In a heart-wrenching moment, Morgan puts his wife in his rifle sights...but he cannot bring himself to pull the trigger. Both of these scenarios express the central theme of *The Walking Dead* (which, by the way, was communicated from the very first scene of the pilot): *the struggle to maintain one's humanity in the wake of disaster.* Several seasons later, the series still finds new ways to explore that theme.

THE WALKING DEAD

Pilot "Days Gone Bye" (2010)

Teleplay and Directed by Frank Darabont

Based on graphic novels written by Robert Kirkman

TEASER

1-5 **OPENING**: DEPUTY SHERIFF RICK GRIMES pulls up to a deserted gas station, looking for gas. He spots a little girl walking, from behind. He calls to her and she turns around – she is a zombie! **CATALYST**: He is forced to draw his gun and shoot her in the head. Rick is troubled by this act. (**THEME**: *The struggle to maintain one's humanity in the wake of disaster*.) ("A" STORY: Rick exploring the new world and choosing when to kill.)

[OPENING TITLES. Mood is scary, mysterious, with rising tension.]

ACT ONE

5-9 Rick and his partner SHANE sit in their squad car, sharing lunch and conversation about women. When Shane asks Rick about his wife Lorrie, Rick reveals they're having problems. ("C" Story: The survivor colony with Shane, Lorrie and son Carl) They get a call on the radio about a hot pursuit and race into action.

9-12 Shane, Rick and other COPS set up a blockade on a rural road.

12 **INCITING INCIDENT**: Rick is shot, goes down. FADE OUT.

13 Rick wakes up in a hospital bed, his gunshot wound is bandaged. Curiously, no one is around. The hospital is deserted. He wanders around, sees the mangled, dead body of a nurse on the ground.

18 **TURN**: Rick reaches double exit doors that have been chained shut, with "Don't Open. Dead Inside" spray-painted on the outside. Unseen growling masses push on the door. Gnarled fingers reach out from the crack between the two doors. Rick isn't in Kansas anymore.

HINT AT MORE: How many zombies are there and can Rick survive this new world?

ACT TWO

20-23 **AFTERMATH**: Rick walks around outside the hospital, finding stacks of dead bodies, the detritus of a mass evacuation. The torso of a zombie woman slithers toward him! Terrified, he bolts.

24 **FIRST TRIAL**: Rick comes to his home, to find it empty. He breaks down in sobs, calling out the names of his wife and son.

26 **FIRST CASUALTY**: Outside, Rick is knocked out with a shovel swung by a kid, DWAYNE, who mistook Rick for a zombie. Dwayne's father MORGAN (**Dynamic Ally** and **Shadow**) spares Rick's life. ("B" STORY: Morgan and his wife.)

28 **NEW COMPLICATIONS**: Back at Morgan's house, Rick is tied up. Morgan cuts him loose after some questions, but warns him not to try anything or he'll be forced to use his very sharp buck knife.

30 **MIDPOINT**: Morgan gives Rick vital exposition about the state of the world, the "rules" of the post-zombie plague. They call them "Walkers," and they are more active after dark. They are attracted to noise and light, which is why Morgan and Dwayne have sealed up their home like a bunker where they hide from the Walkers. If they bite or scratch you, you will turn into a Walker, an undead.

34-36 Morgan shows Rick his WIFE, now a Walker, walking in the street outside their home. Dwayne cries at the sight of his undead mom. Morgan is ashamed to admit that he has not had the strength to "put down" his wife. (**New Challenge**: Will Rick be able to kill his family if they are turned into Walkers?)

ACT THREE

37 **Partial Integration (A, B and C)**: Rick, Morgan and Dwayne go back to Rick's house. Rick is sure Lorrie and his son Carl are alive. Morgan mentions a rumor that there is a large survivor colony outside town, and a treatment facility set up by the CDC.

39 **ASSUMPTION OF POWER**: Rick leads them in a raid on the weapons cage at the police station. They stock up on guns and ammo. Rick is setting off on his own to search for his family.

43 Before they separate, Morgan warns Rick about the dangers of coming across a pack of Walkers (setup: Walker mob.).

43 Rick spots a fellow cop (seen in Opening), now a Walker, and knows he must release him from misery. Rick executes him with a merciful shot to the head.

45-48 **SHADOW SHOWDOWN**: Cross-cut montage of Morgan and Rick, both attempting acts of mercy. Morgan lines up his wife in his sights but he can't pull the trigger (End "B" story). Rick returns to find the half-body zombie woman, and after he says "I'm sorry this happened to you" he executes her. (**Rick goes "all in."**)

Hint at more: Rick has lost his innocence; he now shows the strength he will need to survive the terrible ordeal ahead.

ACT FOUR

50 **AFTERMATH**: Rick drives outside town, broadcasting on the emergency channel of his CB radio. His signal is picked up by a colony of survivors in the woods! The group includes Shane, Rick's old partner. Shane loses Rick on the CB and argues with a woman about going outside the camp to help others.

53 **INTEGRATION (A & C stories)**: Shane and the woman kiss, and we cut back to Rick looking at a photo of his family and realize the woman is LORRIE, his wife. Shane is now in a relationship with her, and acting as surrogate father to Rick's son, CARL. (End "C" story)

54 **Skirmishes and Complications**: Rick runs out of gas. He travels to a country home to find a couple dead of suicide by shotgun. Rick finds a horse!

57 **NEW BEGINNING/DECLARATION OF WAR**: Rick mounts up, looking very much like an old west sheriff. He rides the horse into Atlanta, a ghost town.

60 **ALL IS LOST**: Rick runs into a massive mob of Walkers! (Payoff: Walker mob) He falls off the horse, which they quickly make into lunch.

ACT FIVE

60-66 **CLIMAX ("A" story)**: Rick makes a harrowing escape, climbing into a tank. A voice on the radio calls him "the dumbass in the tank." Has Rick found a new ally or foe?

66 FADE OUT on the final image of hundreds of hungry Walkers converging on the tank.

CLIFFHANGER: How will Rick survive? Who is the voice on the radio?

GAME OF THRONES PILOT
"WINTER IS COMING"

Written By David Benioff & D.B. Weiss

Game Of Thrones is a sprawling, epic serial set in a fantasy world of swords and sorcery, about the unending battle for supremacy in the Seven Kingdoms of Westeros. Like *The Lord of the Rings* before it, the series draws on rich source material (the novels of George R.R. Martin) filled with many lands, colorful characters and fantastic creatures. Unlike *The Lord of the Rings*, there is plenty of bloodshed and copious nudity. Which may seem like a frivolous observation, but it is actually crucial to the show's success that it targeted an adult audience, thus setting itself apart from the many fantasy films aimed at a "family" audience (e.g., *Rings, Harry Potter*, etc.). One of the keys to television's success in the past decade has been the ability to provide entertainment that cannot be found on the big screen. Interestingly, *Thrones* aims for big screen scale and production values (including top-notch CGI) but where it really differentiates itself from feature films is in character development.

This is a true multi-protagonist pilot. The central characters or "co-protagonists" – those with the most screen time and the deepest arcs – are Ned Stark, Jon Snow and Daenerys "Dany" Targaeryen. They are each pressured to make life-changing decisions. Interestingly, Ned is the only one to truly make a decision, although it is offscreen: he accepts King Barratheon's request to become the Hand, the second most powerful position in royalty. Dany is passive, and Jon has yet to commit to joining the Night's Watch (this happens at the end of the second episode).

The creators can get away with largely passive main characters because the pilot is all about <u>world-building</u>. It is more about the promise of high adventure than the delivery of it. And yet, the writers use active devices to move the story; they *show* more than tell. We can clearly see the seeds of conflict being sown. We know this story will sprawl.

The structure of "Winter is Coming" is kept rather simple. The first three Act openings are clearly delineated by location – Winterfell, King's Landing and Pentos – in Act Three we begin to cross-cut between Winterfell and Pentos. Along the way, we are dropping hints of struggles for birthright, military alliances and even incest. There are several mentions of history and how that informs the present. We will come to find out that history repeats itself in this deadly game of thrones.

With such extensive source material to draw from, the creators of *Game of Thrones* could tease certain aspects that would not truly come into play for many more episodes. Dany's dragon eggs won't hatch until the final episode of season one and the dragons won't grow larger than her until Season Four. The White Walkers glimpsed in the cold open of the pilot's Teaser (which I still think is too slow) will appear only a few times in the next three seasons.

This slower pace affects the Beat Sheet. The true Inciting Incident of the pilot (the death of John Arryn) does not occur until Act Two, 18 minutes in. We wait until Act Three to establish our third co-protagonist, Daenerys, who I label as the "B" story because she has the second most screen time behind Ned Stark.

At the time of this writing, the show is still going strong and there is no reason to believe it will end any time soon. Many series nowadays end after six or seven seasons to preserve quality and audience share, but *Game of Thrones*, with its dense source material and ever-evolving cast of characters, could continue well beyond that marker. It will be fun to see how the ride continues, and to find out who claims that throne, after all.

GAME OF THRONES

Pilot "Winter is Coming" (2011)

Written By David Benioff & D.B. Weiss / Directed by Tim Van Patten

Based on "A Song of Ice and Fire" by George R.R. Martin

TEASER

1-4 **OPENING**: A party of three RANGERS from the Night's Watch exits the massive frozen wall and rides South on a mission. YOUNG RANGER walks ahead, finding a massacre of dead bodies. He and the SECOND RANGER want to return to the castle, but their CAPTAIN refuses to leave.

5-7 **CATALYST**: They are attacked by WHITE WALKERS! The zombie-like creatures kill the Captain and the Second Ranger. As the Young Ranger trembles, waiting for death, we FADE OUT.

[OPENING TITLES]

ACT ONE

8 **AFTERMATH**: The Young Ranger is found, wandering the countryside, and taken into custody by soldiers.

9 TITLE: <u>WINTERFELL</u>. **OPENING**: We meet the Stark family. Lord NED STARK, his wife CATELYN, sons ROBB, JON, and BRAN, daughters SANSA and ARYA, and ward THEON GREYJOY. They teach young Bran (our **New Arrival**) to shoot his bow, but even younger Arya, a tomboy, is already better than Bran.

11 ("A" Story: Ned's honor) Ned is told about the Young Ranger, considered a deserter from the Night's Watch, a crime punishable by death. Catelyn objects, but Ned knows it is his duty to put this man to death.

12-15 Beheading ceremony. ("C" Story: Jon Snow's place in the family) Jon tells Bran not to look away as Ned beheads the Young Ranger.

16 **TURN ("A" Story)**: They find dead animals, mysteriously killed by a powerful predator. Jon Snow convinces Ned to spare the pups of a dead Dire Wolf. It could be an omen, as there are five pups, one for each of the Stark children. **TURN ("C" Story):** Theon laughingly gives Jon the "runt of the litter," because Jon is not actually a Stark.

ACT TWO

17-19 TITLE: <u>KINGS LANDING</u>. ("D" Story: Jaime and Cersei) **INCITING INCIDENT ("A" & "D")**: In the castle, a funeral is being held for John Arryn, the former "Hand of the King." We meet the royal siblings, JAIME and CERSEI LANNISTER. Cersei wants Jaime to be the next Hand, but he doesn't want the job; it's too much work and too dangerous.

20-22 Back in Winterfell, Catelyn (**Dynamic Ally**) tells Ned the news that John Arryn has died. Arryn was like a father to Ned. **New Complications**: The King is coming for a visit! They must prepare.

23-24 Catelyn rebukes Bran for climbing up the tower. He could hurt himself (Setup for "D" Story climax). Arya is also fooling around. These are two mischievous kids.

25-28 **FIRST TRIAL**: The royal family from King's Landing arrives at Winterfell: KING ROBERT BARRATHEON, JOFFREY the boy prince, Cersei and Jaime. Arya asks, "Where is the imp?"

29 **MIDPOINT**: Robert asks Ned to be his Hand of the King and wants their children to wed, joining their houses. Ned has a great weight on his shoulders.

30-31 **FIRST CASUALTY**: We meet TYRION the "imp" (he's a dwarf) in the whore house with a concubine. Jaime brings three more whores for his baby brother with a reminder to attend the feast later.

32 **SHADOW SHOWDOWN**: King Robert and Ned visit Ned's sister's tomb. Robert was to wed her, his true love, before she was murdered by the Targaryens. Ned says the Targaryens are gone. Robert says "not all of them."

ACT THREE

33-35 TITLE: <u>PENTOS</u>. **FIRST TRIAL/FIRST CASUALTY**: ("B" Story: Daenerys marries Kal Drogo) Meet DAENERYS TARGAREYN and her insufferable brother, VESERYS TARGAREYN. They have been exiled from their homeland (where they were royalty) for one year. He expects to return and regain his crown soon. He undresses and fondles her.

36-37 **INCITING INCIDENT ("B")**: KAL DROGO and his Dothraki warriors ride up. Veserys has arranged for Dany to wed Kal. Kal looks at Dany then rides off, giving no indication of his feelings.

38-39 **SHADOW SHOWDOWN**: Dany tries to get her brother to let her out of the marriage, but he refuses because they need the Dothraki army to take back the crown. Dany has no say in her own destiny.

40 Back in Winterfell, Catelyn speaks with her eldest daughter, Sansa. Sansa begs her to ask Ned to say yes to the King's offer to become The Hand so she can wed Prince Joffrey.

40 **INTEGRATION**: Banquet with the two families.

Outside, UNCLE BENJI (Jon's **Dynamic Ally**) rides up, greets Jon. **ASSUMPTION OF POWER ("C")**: Jon asks him if he can join the Night's Watch. Benji warns him about the tough life of a Watchman—it is a lifelong oath, wherein they swear off marriage and family.

41-43 **SHADOW SHOWDOWN**: Tyrion talks to Jon about being "a bastard." Jon's father is Ned Stark but his mother was a lover of Ned's, not Catelyn. Tyrion may be a full-blooded Lannister but, as a dwarf, he is the outcast of his family. (End "C" story)

45 Sansa greets Cersei in front of Catelyn. Cersei insults Catelyn's homeland.

46 **ASSUMPTION OF POWER ("D")**: Jaime and Ned trade barbs (foreshadowing their fight in episode 5). Arya flings food at her sister, gets in trouble with her mother.

48-50 **TURN**: Urgent message from a rider from Catelyn's sister: Jon

Arryn was murdered by the Lannisters and the king is in danger!
ROADBLOCK: Catelyn begs Ned not to take the job while MAESTER
LUWIN tells Ned he must—he swore an oath.

> MAESTER LUWIN
>
> If this news is true and the
> Lannisters conspire against the
> throne, who but you can protect
> the throne?

> CATELYN STARK
>
> They murdered the last Hand, now
> you want Ned to take the job?

> MAESTER LUWIN
>
> The king rode for a month to ask
> Lord Stark's help. He's the only
> one he trusts. You swore the king
> an oath, my Lord.

> CATELYN STARK
>
> He spent half his life fighting
> Robert's wars. He owes him
> nothing. Your father and brother
> rode south once, on a king's
> demand.

> MAESTER LUWIN
>
> A different time. A different
> king.

(This discussion touches on the theme of the first season, *the damage caused by the unquenchable thirst for power*, and it foreshadows how Ned's sense of honor and tradition will do nothing to save him from treachery.)

ALL IS LOST: What choice will Ned make?

ACT FOUR

50-52 Dothraki wedding reception for Kal and Dany. Public sex acts and fights to the death are the highlights of this event. (Downton Abbey this is not!) Dany is uncomfortable and scared. SIR JORAH MORMONT (Dany's **Dynamic Ally**) greets Dany and brings her gifts. He is a former servant of her father. She immediately takes to him, but Veserys doesn't trust him.

53-54 Dany is gifted <u>three dragon eggs</u>, told they are merely rocks now.

55-57 **CLIMAX ("B")**: Dany rides off on a white horse with Kal. Kal forces her to have sex on a cliff-side facing the ocean. She begins to cry. (End "B" story)

ACT FIVE

57-58 **CLIMAX ("A")**: Ned rides off with the King to go on a hunt. <u>Ned has accepted the position</u>. (End "A" Story)

58-60 **CLIMAX ("C")**: Bran climbs the tower again. He reaches the top floor, comes upon Sir Jaime Lannister having sex...with his sister Cersei. Jaime pushes Bran out the window! As Bran falls from the high tower, we CUT TO BLACK.

BREAKING BAD "PILOT"

Written By Vince Gilligan

Breaking Bad has an incredibly tight pilot episode, consisting of several economical 2-minute scenes in a Teaser plus five act structure. This wasn't always the case. If you've read the original script, you'll notice that a number of trims were made before air. The result is a near-perfect example of the Beat Sheet template.

At 57 minutes, the pilot episode is long for a basic-cable network show with commercials, but it flies by because we are constantly meeting interesting characters as we are taken into this new, dangerous, yet thrilling world. I love how everyone has their own particular "voice" in dialogue. There's the macho DEA brother-in-law, the teenage son with cerebral palsy, the former student turned drug dealer, the Middle-Eastern car wash owner, etc.

The story is told from Walt's POV – we discover things as he does. He undergoes a dramatic arc from start to finish, which is not always the case in pilots, which sometimes center on a character who is unwavering in their view of the world and unchanged by episode's end. This emphasis on change was built into creator Vince Gilligan's plan from the start; in fact, he even gives Walt the line, "Chemistry is the study of change," a not-so-subtle clue of the crucible to come.

The era of the anti-hero may have already been in full swing when *Breaking Bad* debuted, but those dark protagonists (e.g., Tony Soprano, Vic Mackey, Al Swearingen) were *always* bad. Walt's radical transformation (the "Mr. Chips to Scarface" arc) was gradual, and unheard of in previous generations of television. One can't imagine Jim Rockford of *The Rockford Files* or Noah Wyle on *E.R.* turning into unforgivable monsters. By series' end, Walt's arc had become so popular with audiences that AMC couldn't help but greenlight the story of the transformation of another key character from the *Breaking Bad* universe; thus, *Better Call Saul* was born.

BREAKING BAD

"Pilot" (2008)

Written and Directed by Vince Gilligan

TEASER

1-3 **OPENING**: A man in his underwear wearing a gas mask, WALTER WHITE, drives an RV with three unconscious men inside the car. ("A" story: Walt's meth business) Walter crashes the RV, gets out and records a first-person message into a video camera to his family, Skyler and Walter Junior: "No matter how it may look, I only had you in my heart."

CATALYST: Walt points a gun at oncoming sirens.

ACT ONE

4-6 Walt wakes up, exercises. We see awards on the wall for science achievements. He wife SKYLER gives him his 50th birthday breakfast, with veggie bacon, no cholesterol...yippee. ("B" Story: Walt's family) Skyler tells him to leave at 5:00, don't let his boss dick him around again. Their son WALTER, JR., who has cerebral palsy, clashes with Skyler. She's clearly the authority in the household.

7-8 Walt teaches high school chemistry to lethargic teenagers. Chemistry is the "study of change." The cycle of life. Growth...decay...transformation. (Foreshadowing of Walter White's epic character arc.) Punk kid CHAD makes a scene, Walt fails to discipline him.

9-10 Walt works the register at a Car Wash. His boss BAGDAN makes him wash cars when an employee quits. Walt coughs. Chad takes a photo of him washing his car. How humiliating.

11-13 Walt comes home to a surprise 50th birthday party! We learn Skyler is pregnant and her sister MARIE is a bitch. **Dynamic Ally***: Marie's husband HANK, a DEA agent, shows off his gun, impressing Walter Jr. ("C" Story: Hank) Hank gives Walt a hard time in jest, then offers a toast to Walt, the smartest guy he knows. **INCITING**

INCIDENT: Hank turns on the TV so everyone can see a news interview he gave after his team made a big meth lab sting. Walt is impressed that the DEA nabbed $700,000 in dirty cash.

*NOTE: Although Hank will go on to become an Antagonist and Shadow to Walt throughout the series, in the pilot he is essentially an ally in that he facilitates Walt getting into the meth business with Jesse. Jesse will become a Dynamic Ally later on, but in the pilot he is Walt's Shadow because he is the polar opposite of Walt in every way (age, home life, career, morals, etc.) and his incompetence creates major obstacles for Walt.

14-15 In bed that night, Skyler gives Walt a special birthday hand job as she reads on her laptop. As he gets worked up, she also gets excited...for her eBay sale.

16-17 **TURN**: Next day, Walt collapses at the car wash.

ACT TWO

17-18 **AFTERMATH**: The Doctor tells Walt he has inoperable lung cancer. With chemo, he'll live maybe another couple years. Walt is in a daze.

19-20 **COMPLICATIONS ("A" and "B")**: Skyler and Walt are having money problems. Walt doesn't tell Skyler he's sick. At the car wash, Walt explodes, tells Bagdan to fuck off and storms out.

21 Walt throws matches into the pool, depressed. Calls Hank to set up the ride-along he mentioned at the party.

22-25 **FIRST TRIAL**: Walt rides along with Hank as they take down the meth lab of the infamous "Cap'n Cook." Walt is fascinated by the lab equipment.

26 **FIRST CASUALTY**: Walt spots JESSE PINKMAN (**Shadow**), his former student, escaping the scene. Jesse drives off in his car, license plate: "THE CAPN!"

27-30 **MIDPOINT**: Walt blackmails Jesse to partner with him to make and sell meth, or he'll turn him in.

ACT THREE

30-31 Skyler with Marie at home, boxing items for Ebay.

32-35 Walt steals chemistry equipment from school storage, brings it to Jesse's house. **SHADOW SHOWDOWN**: They immediately clash as Jesse tells him his meth is "art," not chemistry. Walt insists on proper scientific methods and safety, muscling Jesse. Jesse suggests buying an RV from his friend.

36-37 **ASSUMPTION OF POWER ("A" Story)**: Walt empties his savings to pay for the RV. $7,000. Jesse asks him to level with him: Why is he doing this? Walt says "I am awake."

38-39 **ASSUMPTION OF POWER ("B" Story)**: Walt and Skyler with Junior at a clothing store, helping him try on jeans. When a group of kids make fun of Junior, Walt goes nuts and takes out the head bully. Walt is a bad-ass!

ACT FOUR

40-43 **Skirmishes and Complications**: In desert, in the RV. Walt works in his underwear so his clothes don't smell of chemicals; Jesse mocks him. Chemistry montage – Walt is serious and Jesse is unfocused. Jesse proclaims their product "art!" Jesse wants to sample it, but Walt stops him. This is serious work, not party time. The next step is selling it, and that's Jesse's department.

44-46 Jesse at Chris's (KRAZY-8) home, looking to set up a deal. Krazy-8 is the cousin of Emilio, Jesse's old partner who was arrested by Hank in the seizure witnessed by Walt. Emilio just got out of jail and is pissed at Jesse, thinking he ratted on him.

47-48 **TURN**: Back in the desert as Walt is cooking in the RV. Krazy-8, Emilio and Jesse pull up. **INTEGRATION (A & C):** Emilio recognizes Walt from Hank's DEA sting, thinks he's a cop. They pull guns on Walt and Jesse! **ALL IS LOST**: Desperate, Walt offers to teach them his recipe if they spare their lives.

ACT FIVE

49-51 **BIG RISK/DECLARATION OF WAR**: Walt cooks for Emilio and Krazy-8, with Jesse tied up outside. In a bold move, he makes a bomb with red phosphorus and takes out the gangsters! He unties Jesse, puts a gas mask on him and drives like mad out of there. We are BACK AT THE OPENING SEQUENCE FROM THE TEASER...

52-54 **CLIMAX ("A")**: Walt with the gun aimed as sirens approach. He puts the gun to his chin, pulls the trigger...nothing. He can't even kill himself. He puts up his arms, sobbing, waiting for the police to take him...but it's the fire department. **BIG WIN**: They drive right past him! He's safe.

55-57 **CLIMAX ("B")**: Walt dries his cash in the dryer. In bed, Skyler asks him not to shut her out; to talk to her. **NEW WORLD**: He makes passionate love to her, in stark contrast to the lame hand job scene earlier. Skyler asks, "Walt, is that you?" Walter White is a new man.

CLIFFHANGER: Will Walt tell his wife about his side job?

HOUSE OF CARDS PILOT
"CHAPTER 1"

Written By Beau Willimon

House of Cards was the first major one-hour drama series to come from a streaming provider, in this case, Netflix. It paved the way for future Netflix series like *Orange is the New Black*, *Bloodline* and *Daredevil*, and ensured that online platforms would be taken seriously by the industry and audiences, alike.

When Kevin Spacey won the Emmy for his gripping, frightening performance of Senator Frank Underwood, it signaled a watershed moment in television. Netflix, Amazon and their ilk were now players in the game, just as basic cable networks like AMC and FX had fought their way out of the shadows of the major networks with breakout hits like *Mad Men* and *Sons of Anarchy*.

From the get-go, the producers of *House of Cards* were swinging for the fences. With a huge budget, big screen talent and cinematic production values, the goal was to deliver a TV series that was indistinguishable from a feature film.

The pilot script for *House of Cards* was written like a feature screenplay, and the resulting episode was helmed by well-known feature director David Fincher. The episode looks and feels like an R-rated drama film, yet it promises a sprawling story we can get lost in for days. The script did not contain labeled act breaks, but the structure clearly follows the classic TV drama structure discussed in this book, so I've inserted my own act breaks below in what feel like the natural positions.

HOUSE OF CARDS

Pilot "Chapter One" (2013)

Written by Beau Willimon / Directed by David Fincher

TEASER

1 **OPENING**: A dog is hit by a car outside the home of Senator
FRANCIS "FRANK" UNDERWOOD. Frank orders his bodyguard to find
the owners as he consoles the crippled pooch. He speaks into the
camera...

>   FRANCIS
> There are two kinds of pain, the
> sort of pain that makes you
> strong or useless pain. The sort
> of pain that is only suffering,
> the sort of pain that's useless.
> I have no patience for useless
> things. Moments like this require
> someone who will act, do the
> unpleasant thing. The necessary
> thing.
>   (chokes the dog)
> There. No more pain.

2-3 **WORLD**: Frank and his wife CLAIRE attend a New Year's Eve party
hosted by President-elect GARRET WALKER. ("A" Story: Frank's master
plan.) Walker is Frank's ticket up the ranks so he can rise above House
Majority Whip. **CATALYST**: Frank got Walker's Chief of Staff, LINDA
VASQUEZ hired, and now he expects her to return the favor. Give and
take. Welcome to Washington.

4-5 [OPENING TITLES.]

ACT ONE

5-6 On the limo ride home, we learn Claire runs a non-profit and is also
very ambitious. ("D" Story: Claire's non-profit.) She wants Frank to
help her procure a large donation from Sancorp. She says, "This is

going to be a big year for us."

6-7 **New Arrival** and **Shadow**: ZOE BARNES, young cub reporter at *The Washington Herald*. ("B" Story: Zoe's rise as a reporter.) She tries to convince her editor LUCAS to promote her. She wants to "lift the veil" on Washington.

7-9 **Dynamic Ally**: PETER RUSSO, young Senator, meets with an angry union guy who wants the zoning laws that Russo promised in his election. ("C" Story: Peter's decline.) Peter fakes a call from the President-elect but it's actually from his secretary/mistress, CHRISTINA, who talks dirty to him.

9-11 **INCITING INCIDENT**: Linda Vasquez breaks the news to Frank that they are not nominating him for Secretary of State. Frank is livid but puts on a positive face, agrees to stand by them. Michael Kern is their choice over Frank.

11-12 Claire at her environmental firm. She is excited for their new direction, to be hiring new people. She calls Frank but gets his voicemail.

13- Zoe is rebuffed by JANINE, a senior reporter.

14-15 **FIRST TRIAL/FIRST CASUALTY**: When Frank tells Claire about his passing-over, she dresses him down for not returning her calls and for underestimating Vasquez and Walker. She won't accept his apologies.

>   CLAIRE
>   My husband doesn't apologize.
>   Even to me.

16-18 **TURN & DECISION**: Later, Frank and Claire reconcile and agree to dedicate to a plan of action that will take them to the top.

>   FRANCIS
>   I love that woman. I love her
>   more than sharks love blood.

HINT AT MORE: How will they work together?

ACT TWO

18-19 **AFTERMATH**: Frank lays out a plan with his right hand man, DOUG STAMPER. First, they will take out Kern, then hand-pick his replacement. They need an errand boy, someone who they can control completely.

25-26 Zoe researches Frank.

27-28 **MIDPOINT**: Vasquez needs the education bill drafted, more centrist, in the first 100 days. Frank takes the job, plans to use it to destroy her.

ACT THREE

29 **AFTERMATH**: Frank's office is bustling. He tells Doug to set up a meeting with Catherine Durant.

30-31 **ROADBLOCK ("D" Story)**: Claire's office. She breaks the news to her office manager EVELYN that they lost Sancorp's donation and Claire needs her to fire half the staff. Evelyn objects, but Claire is adamant.

31-35 **SHADOW SHOWDOWN**: Zoe shows up at Frank's brownstone, talks her way in with sex appeal. They find they have a connection: they are both people who think they are worth more than their current position. She correctly deduces that education is the first agenda of the new administration. He sends her on her way.

35-36 **COMPLICATIONS**: Peter is pulled over, drunk, with a hooker in his car. He is arrested.

37 Frank sends Doug to meet with the POLICE COMMISSIONER and offer their help for him to become Mayor if he lets Peter Russo free.

38 **TURN:** Peter is bailed out, lies to Christina that he was alone.

38 Claire asks Frank for two more tickets to the ball for potential investors. She's happy he's making progress.

39 **ASSUMPTION OF POWER**: In his office, Frank shreds the

education bill in front of its author, DONALD BLITHE. Frank is manipulating Blithe well so as to eliminate him.

ACT FOUR

40 Frank meets with CATHERINE DURANT, offering her Kern's position of Secretary of State. She is dubious but intrigued. He asks for her trust in him.

41 Doug recovers the half-shredded education bill from the trash dumpster.

42-43 **INTEGRATION ("A" & "B"):** Zoe meets Frank in a museum. He tests her to prove she has the chops to be an effective ally.

43 **DECLARATION OF WAR ("A"):** Frank leaks the shredded education bill to Zoe. She stays up late writing her story.

44 Vasquez is frustrated with Frank, but he assures her that he can work with Blithe and make the 100 days deadline. Asks for two extra tickets to the Jefferson Ball (as per Claire's request). **ALL IS LOST**: Frank's plan is getting more complicated, may be derailed by Vasquez.

45-46 **CLIMAX ("C")**: Frank reveals to Peter that he was the one who bailed him out of jail and blackmails him for his absolute loyalty. (End "C" Story)

47-49 **CLIMAX ("B"):** Zoe delivers the education bill and her analysis to her editor. Janine is given second billing to Zoe. (End "B" Story)

ACT FIVE

49-50 **NEW WORLD:** Frank sits 15 feet from President Walker as he is inaugurated. Walker pledges to deliver a comprehensive education bill in the first 100 days.

50-51 Inaugural Ball. Frank schmoozes, dancing with Catherine, wooing her.

52-54 **CLIMAX ("A")**: Next morning, Frank eats ribs for breakfast at FREDDY's restaurant as we see Zoe Barnes' exposé of the education bill on the front page of the *Washington Herald*. A montage shows the impact on all the players. Heads will certainly roll, and the first stage of Frank's plan is complete. A young man is arrested for the canine hit and run (from the Teaser). Frank orders another rack of ribs.

                    FRANCIS
          I'm feeling hungry today.

MAD MEN PILOT
"SMOKE GETS IN YOUR EYES"

Written By Matthew Weiner

When the first episode of Matthew Weiner's *Mad Men* premiered on July 19, 2007 on the AMC channel, the network had previously been known only for showing old movies. It ushered in a re-branding of the network as a producer of original, serialized content, paving the way for *Breaking Bad* and *The Walking Dead* and providing a template for other cable networks to get into the scripted TV business.

The beat sheet below is based on the completed pilot episode. The episode is 48 minutes long and the script was 52 pages in length. The script does not contain act markers, but it contains three FADE OUTS that correspond to what I assume were commercial breaks. I initially used them as guides for the map, but the episode's structure departed from the script, so I found myself going through several iterations before finally arriving at four acts, no teaser, which gives it the least number of acts of our eight case studies. In a unique move, Weiner ends the "A" story at the close of Act Two, leaving acts three and four to the more character-driven B, C and D stories. This is not the only way it breaks with convention, ultimately distinguishing itself as a masterwork.

This pilot does not contain a ton of plot, but it works fabulously because it emphasizes the voices of its characters, the theme and the very particular setting. It's building a world that we want to spend more time in, if for no other reason than to bask in the witty repartee. It's all about dialogue, which is all about the theme, *It's a man's world.* As the series goes on, the primary theme will become *the pursuit of happiness in an increasingly cynical and chaotic world.* But Weiner knew that a pilot's first job is to suck in the reader/viewer, so he went bold with his first episode, pouring on the sexism and stylized dialogue as strong as the booze in a Sterling Cooper liquor cart.

In keeping with the period of the beginning of the Sixties, all of the main characters are striving to become something new, to escape the positions that society has thrust upon them. The ad campaigns reflect this theme, with Rachel Menken trying to convince a bunch of WASPs that she's "not just another Jewish department store," and the Lucky Strike boys hoping to stand out from their competition amidst the stigma that their product causes cancer. The dynamic between Pete Campbell and Don Draper is particularly interesting, and their character construction is clearly built on dualities. Pete is Don's "Shadow," not only in social background but on the job, as Pete is in Accounts but wishes he was in Creative like Don. He even says as much with the line, "I'm not going to pretend I don't want your job," and he tries to shake Don's hand, to which Don replies, "Let's slow down, I don't want to wake up pregnant."

If you've seen the show and you know Don's secret, it's interesting to look back at the early episodes and you may just see a subtext of "acting" in many of the scenes, not just in Jon Hamm's performance but in the character's dialogue and actions. He's not who he says he is, and this fascinating game of pretend he's playing (perhaps his true Achilles Heel) informs his character for seven seasons of powerful drama. From a distance, we can see that Don's journey is just one big ticking time clock, counting down to the moment when he can no longer sell the façade, when the actor can no longer play the part.

MAD MEN

Pilot "Smoke Gets In Your Eyes" (2007)

Written By Matthew Weiner / Directed by Alan Taylor

1 Titles and Opening Card:

MAD MEN

*A term coined in the late 1950's to describe
the advertising executives of Madison Avenue.*

They coined it.

ACT ONE

1-3 **OPENING**: DON DRAPER asks a black waiter why he smokes Old Gold cigarettes. "I love smoking." Don's trying to figure it out. ("A" story: Don's pitch)

3-6 Visits MIDGE, his sexy girlfriend, late at night. A recent anti-cigarette article in *Reader's Digest* has caused a stir. Don has NOTHING. They sleep together. The next morning, Don says, "We should get married." It's nine hours until his meeting with the tobacco people.

7-8 **CATALYST**: Young ad guys hitting on **New Arrival**, PEGGY. ("C" Story: Peggy's first day on the job) The guys are excited about the upcoming bachelor party for PETE CAMPBELL. ("B" Story: Pete's bachelor party)

8-10: JOAN shows Peggy the ropes. Joan: "They want something between a mother and a waitress." All about sex, looks and hooking a man to live in the country. Joan introduces Peggy to her new boss, Don.

10-12 **Dynamic Ally**: ROGER asks Don about his Lucky Strike pitch. Roger needs a Jew for the Menken's Department Store meeting. Don left in office, alone, he's got nothing. We see his purple heart, Lt. Don Draper.

12-15 SAL, closeted gay art director, playing up the fake libido.

German woman researcher, GRETA, says Freud's "death wish" is the way to approach the medical issues with cigarettes. Don throws her report in the trash.

16-17 Don sleeps in his office, the sounds of battle in his head (A hint at Don's "ghost:" His military service). Peggy wakes him. After Pete is a giant asshole to her, Don dresses Pete down.

18-19 **INCITING INCIDENT:** Don meets a new client, RACHEL MENKEN: "You were expecting a man." (**ROADBLOCK**: Don must be subordinate to a woman.) ("D" story: Don and Rachel Menken) Roger got a Jewish employee from the mailroom to pose as an artist to make Rachel and co. more comfortable.

CLIFFHANGER: Can Don work for a woman?

ACT TWO

20-22 Peggy at the doctor getting the pill, doctor warns her not to be a "strumpet" and not to abuse the medicine. "Even in our modern times, easy women don't find husbands."

22-24 **FIRST TRIAL**: Don and team pitch Menken. She criticizes their approach. **FIRST CASUALTY**: Don flies into a rage: "I'm not going to let a woman talk to me like this. This meeting is over." He storms out.

25 **SHADOW SHOWDOWN**: Pete appeals to Don to help him out. Don: "Let's take it a little slower, I don't want to wake up pregnant." Pete fumes.

25-26 Joan introduces Peggy to the phone pool. One of the girls is the third person to tell Peggy to show off her legs. Maybe this job is really just about sex.

27-32 **MIDPOINT**: Lucky Strike meeting with the Garners. Negative press and lawsuits are killing them; they need a dynamic new campaign. Don still has nothing. Pete brings out research from Don's trash. Americans have a death wish? It bombs and the Garners get up to leave. **(ALL IS LOST "A")** As they leave, Lee says, "At least we know that if we have this problem, everyone has this problem," and Don suddenly gets inspired and turns it into his **ASSUMPTION OF**

POWER ("A" Story): He comes up with a way that they can differentiate themselves from their competition...the tag line "It's toasted!"

>   DON DRAPER
> Advertising is based on one
> thing. Happiness. And you know
> what happiness is? Happiness is
> the smell of a new car, it's
> freedom from fear, it's a bill-
> board on the side of the road
> that screams, whatever you're
> doing is okay. You are okay.

The Garners buy it. (End "A" Story)

(<u>Note</u>: Notice how the "It's toasted" campaign works by pointing out the one way in which this product can be different from the other, identical products, which brilliantly reflects the era the series will explore, as the cookie-cutter middle class ideal of the 1950s breaks down during a decade in which notions of self will radically change. Peggy, Rachel, Sal, Pete and Don are all "hiding in plain sight." They are either not who they seem to be or they are fighting being just another cog in the machine. It should also be noted that this is the same type of "theme sharpening" beat as seen in *Scandal*.)

ACT THREE

33 After the Lucky Strike win, Roger asks Don to do the presidential campaign.

>   ROGER
> Consider the product: young,
> handsome Navy hero. It shouldn't
> be too hard to convince America
> that Dick Nixon is a winner.

34-36 The guys invite Don to Pete's bachelor party, but Don passes. He confronts Pete about stealing Greta's research report from his trash can. **(ALL IS LOST "B")** Peggy makes an awkward pass at Don. **(ALL**

IS LOST "C")

36-38 The bachelor party is in full swing at a strip club. The guys are joined by some girls, and Pete scares one of them off. More rejection, he stews.

38-42 **CLIMAX ("D" Story)**: At a restaurant, Don woos Rachel Menken over drinks, but his charm isn't working. He asks her why she isn't married.

                    RACHEL
          For a lot of people, love isn't
          just a slogan.

                    DON
          The reason you haven't felt it is
          because it doesn't exist. What
          you call love was invented by
          guys like me to sell nylons.
          You're born alone and you die
          alone and this world just drops a
          bunch of rules on you to make you
          forget those facts. But I don't
          forget. I'm living like there's
          no tomorrow, because there isn't
          one.

                    RACHEL
          I don't know what it is you
          really believe in, but I know
          what it's like to be out of
          place...disconnected. There's
          something about you that tells me
          you know it, too.

He's taken aback. She says he's charmed her. She will see him Monday morning for a "real meeting." (End "D" Story)

ACT FOUR

43-45 **CLIMAX & INTEGRATION ("B" & "C"):** Pete shows up drunk at Peggy's door. She takes him in. (End "B" & "C" Story)

45-48 **EPILOGUE/BIG ENDING**: Don goes home to his wife and kids.

APPENDIX:
TV PILOT STORY MAP
WORKSHEET

Use this worksheet to map out your pilot or your template series.

If you would like a Word document of this worksheet emailed to you, please email me at dan@actfourscreenplays.com.

See **The Beat Sheet** for a refresher on the key attributes of each act's signpost beats.

Remember, this is not an exact science. Once you get to the Beat Sheet, you are not bound to the exact ordering, as presented below. As you can see from the **Case Studies** above, the professionals have utilized variations on the Story Map Beat Sheet from time to time. Fulfill as many of the beats as you can, then I suggest you compile a complete scene list, and don't forget to write the script. The true test will come once you complete a few drafts of your pilot.

BASIC STORY MAP

SERIES

TITLE: _____

THEME: _____

_____

_____

COMPELLING CRISIS (OF SERIES): _____

_____

_____

WEEK TO WEEK (OF SERIES): _____

_____

_____

SETTING/WORLD: _____

_____

PROTAGONIST: _____

- Defining Characteristic: _____

- Skill: _____

- Misbehavior: _____

- Achilles Heel/Flaw: _____

PILOT

External Goal: _____

Internal Goal: _____

Central Conflict/Antagonist: _____

Dynamic Ally: _____

Shadow Character: _____

Ending: _____

Pilot Arc: _____

Season One Arc (Optional): _____

Series Arc (Optional): _____

FULL STORY MAP

PILOT STORIES:

"A" Story: _____

_____

_____

"B" Story: _____

_____

_____

"C" Story: _____

_____

_____

"D" Story (Optional): _____

_____

_____

PILOT BEAT SHEET:

TEASER (2-10 PAGES):

- Strong Opening Image: _____

  _____

- Dynamic Opening Sequence: _____

  _____

- Framing Device: _____

  _____

- Fascinating Protagonist: _____

  _____

- World: _____

  _____

- Theme expressed: _____

  _____

- Central Conflict ("A" Story): _____

  _____

- CATALYST: _____

_____

_____

Cliffhanger... _____

_____

ACT ONE (12-15 pages):

- "A" Story: _____

  _____

  _____

- "B" Story: _____

  _____

- "C" Story: _____

  _____

- New Arrival/New World: _____

  _____

- Shadow Character intro'd: _____

  _____

- Dynamic Ally intro'd: _____

  _____

- Theme integrated: _____

  _____

- Escalating Conflict/Stakes: _____

_____

_____

- INCITING INCIDENT: _____

_____

_____

- TURN/Roadblock/Crisis to "A" story: _____

_____

_____

  Cliffhanger... _____

_____

ACT TWO (6-10 pages):

- Aftermath of Cliffhanger: _____

  _____

- FIRST TRIAL: _____

  _____

- FIRST CASUALTY: _____

  _____

- New complications A, B, C: _____

  _____

  _____

- MIDPOINT: _____

  _____

  _____

  New Question/Challenge... _____

  _____

ACT THREE (8-12 pages):

- Aftermath of Midpoint: _____

  _____

- SHADOW SHOWDOWN: _____

  _____

  _____

- Integration of lines: _____

  _____

  _____

- ASSUMPTION OF POWER: _____

  _____

  _____

ACT FOUR (6-12 pages)

- Skirmishes and Complications: _____

    _____

    _____

- Integration, Escalation, Stopping Points: _____

    _____

    _____

- "C" CLIMAX: _____

    _____

- DECLARATION OF WAR: _____

    _____

- ALL IS LOST: _____

    _____

ACT FIVE (2-8 pages):

- "B" CLIMAX: _____

_____

_____

- "A" CLIMAX: _____

_____

_____

- EPILOGUE/ NEW WORLD: _____

_____

_____

- HANGING QUESTION/CLIFFHANGER... _____

_____

_____

ACKNOWLEDGMENTS

I would like to extend my heartfelt thanks to the many individuals who helped me with this book. As always, thank you to my parents for their constant support. Thank you to Joe Nimziki, Larry Reitzer, Fritz Manger, Christine Conradt, Hilary Weisman Graham, Rick Bosner, Jenny Frankfurt, Ben Elterman, Micah Herman, Aaron Goldberg, Lee Stobby, Regina Lee, James Martin, Mike Kim, Tony Mosher, Dustin Tanner, Mike Rozmarin, Kathy Muraviov, Jeanne Bowerman, Aaron Bauer, Shelly Mellott, William Rabkin, Gina Leone, Steve Lam, Leilani Holmes, Guy McDouall and all of the good folks at The Writers Building, The Tracking Board, Inktip, The Blacklist, The Scriptwriters Network and The Writers Store. Thank you to all of the gifted television creators who have entertained and inspired me for decades, to all of my students and clients, and to my partner and muse, Nicole.

Good luck and happy writing!

Dan

Made in the USA
Middletown, DE
14 April 2016